A GIFT FOR

_____

FROM

_____

ASTONISHING
BUT TRUE
SPORTS
STORIES

by
STEVE RIACH

Published by Hallmark Books,
a division of Hallmark Cards, Inc.,
Kansas City, MO 64141
Visit us on the Web at www.Hallmark.com.

Editorial Director: Todd Hafer
Art Director: Kevin Swanson
Design: Gregg & Associates
Composition: Steve Brooker
Production Artist: Dan C. Horton

ISBN: 978-1-59530-204-5

BOK2098

Printed and bound in China

★

ASTONISHING
BUT TRUE
SPORTS
STORIES

by
STEVE RIACH

GIFT BOOKS
from Hallmark

TABLE OF CONTENTS

ASTONISHING
BUT TRUE
BASEBALL
STORIES

CATCH ME IF YOU CAN

Throughout the years, a number of crafty baseball pitchers have discovered numerous ways to doctor the baseball in order to make it move unusually when they throw a pitch. Some have been caught with such illegal substances and items as petroleum jelly, thumbtacks, sandpaper, and various other odds and ends.

One pitcher whom umpires were certain was doctoring the ball was Don Sutton. The Los Angeles Dodgers, Milwaukee Brewers, and California Angels great compiled 323 victories over his career. Yet many felt much of his success had to do with what he did to the ball before he threw it.

One night in 1978, with Sutton on the mound for the Dodgers, umpire Doug Harvey found a foreign substance on the ball during an opponent's at bat. Harvey promptly tossed Sutton from the game. Sutton was livid. He refuted Harvey's claim and threatened to sue Harvey and the other umpires if they ejected him from the game. To placate matters, Harvey informed Sutton that he was being removed from the game because he had thrown a doctored ball. They could not definitively say that Sutton himself had doctored the ball.

Because umpires had never yet been successful in catching Sutton in the act, they were hesitant to waste time and became frustrated. On this occasion, Sutton took everything in stride. When one of the umpiring crew went to the mound to search Sutton's glove for a foreign substance, he instead found a note from the pitcher. It read: "You're getting warm, but it is not here."

MIND GAMES

Hall of Fame catcher Carlton Fisk was known as one of the most talkative men behind the plate in all of baseball. Fisk loved to talk to any batter and any umpire. He was always trying to use his yakking as a means to get a mental edge on the hitter. He sounded innocent, but in fact he was clever.

Longtime umpire Ron Luciano recalls a time in which Fisk got the better of a batter without saying one word to him. It was the conversation with Luciano, who was calling the game behind the plate that night that created the ruse.

Fisk's Boston Red Sox were playing the Cleveland Indians during the summer of the 1976 season. The Indians sent up outfielder Charlie Spikes to pinch hit late in the game. As Spikes stepped into the batter's box, Fisk pretended to continue an ongoing conversation with Luciano.

"You're right, Ronnie, all he wants to do is throw that curveball," Fisk told the umpire of his pitcher, Luis Tiant. Luciano had no idea what Fisk was talking about, so he did not respond.

The first pitch to Tiant was a fastball for a strike, that Spikes watched. Tiant's second pitch was a curveball that was outside for a ball. Fisk jumped up from behind the plate and trotted out to the mound berating the pitcher. Returning to his spot, Fisk muttered to Luciano, "He says he misunderstood the sign."

Now, Luciano recognized that Fisk was setting up Spikes. He could tell Spikes was thinking hard about what was coming next—fastball or curve? Fisk gave Tiant signals for the next pitch, and the pitcher shook him off, which kept Fisk muttering to Luciano. Finally, the next pitch was a curveball that Spikes watched for strike two. Again, Fisk ran out to the mound hollering at Tiant. As he came back this time, Fisk continued to engage Luciano and Spikes. "He says that was a fastball. Now was that a fastball, Ronnie? Of course it wasn't."

At this point, Spikes is in mental knots, not knowing what is coming next. No matter what Tiant threw next, he was not ready to hit it. So Tiant threw a fastball past him for strike three, with Spikes watching once again. During the entire trip to the plate, Spikes had not even moved his bat.

Realizing he had been duped, Spikes turned and let Fisk know what he thought of the gamesmanship. But it was too late, as the ruse had worked; Spikes was out and the Indians threat was over.

BULLPEN

On August 19, 1982, rookie pitcher Pascual Perez was called up from the minor leagues by the Atlanta Braves. The animated, rail-thin Dominican became a legend in Atlanta that day; the day he was to make his major league debut for the Braves in a start against the Montreal Expos.

Perez, a 25-year-old who spoke little English, had qualified for his Georgia driver's license earlier in the day and believed himself self-sufficient enough to find the ballpark on his own without any help. As he attempted to navigate his way around the Atlanta area, he got lost. So he drove around and around and around.

Three times he circled Atlanta on Interstate 285, the highway that loops the metropolitan Atlanta area, each time missing the exit for the stadium. He drove for so long, that at one point he ran out of gas. Realizing that he had no money, he borrowed ten dollars from a gas station attendant to pay for enough gas to make it to the stadium, which he finally did—during the game's second inning.

Durable Braves knuckleball specialist Phil Niekro was called to pitch on a moment's notice and ended up getting the win.

The following night, Perez made it to the park on time and pitched into the 10th inning of a 2–1, extra-innings victory.

Perez's teammates took the incident in stride and determined that in a good-natured sense they would not let him forget his driving escapades. Later that week, Braves players presented Perez with a brand-new warm-up jacket with the number I-285 emblazoned on the back.

SEND ONE TO THE MOON

Pitcher Gaylord Perry was a master of making hitters look foolish. Throughout a major league career that spanned 20 seasons, Perry won Cy Young Awards in both the National and American leagues and won over 300 games. He was an All-Star who played for the San Francisco Giants, Cleveland Indians, San Diego Padres, and New York Yankees.

He is best remembered for how deeply he frustrated hitters. Nearly everyone of his era knew Perry used an illegal substance on the ball to throw a "spitball," but none could ever prove it. Perry was checked by umpires numerous times throughout his career, but was never caught with the goods. Knowing the suggestion of a spitter gave him a mental advantage over hitters, Perry toyed with his opponents. Before every pitch, he entered into a routine of touching his fingers to the bill of his cap, wiping them across the hair behind his ears, and touching them to various parts of his uniform—all spots where Vaseline or some other substance could be concealed. His routine drove hitters crazy. Often, upon striking out on a pitch that moved like a spitter, opposing batters would yell at Perry as they angrily stomped back to the dugout.

For all of Perry's success on the mound, he hardly made a mark at the plate, becoming one of the weakest hitting pitchers of his era. In 1963, as a rookie for the San Francisco Giants, Perry jokingly told the press of his hitting, "They'll put a man on the moon before I hit a home run."

Amazingly, on July 20, 1969, just a few hours after Neil Armstrong became the first man to set foot on the moon, Gaylord Perry hit the first home run of his career.

In 1983, Perry retired with 314 career pitching victories, placing him in the top 20 in baseball history. He also finished with only one lifetime home run.

TOO BIG

Marty Springstead, longtime supervisor and Executive Director of American League umpires, said he will never forget his first assignment as a major league umpire working a game calling balls and strikes behind the plate.

The year was 1966, and Springstead was calling a game involving the Washington Senators at JFK stadium in Washington, D.C.

Bunyunesque slugger Frank Howard was a star for the Senators at the time, and at 6'7" and 250 pounds, he was the game's largest specimen and one of the most fearsome men to step to the plate in all of baseball.

On the first pitch to the mountainous power hitter, Springstead called a knee-high fastball a strike.

Howard turned around and yelled at the rookie umpire. "Get something straight, buster! I don't know where you came from or how you got to the major leagues, but don't call that pitch on me a strike. Understand?"

The next pitch was in the same spot, and Springstead yelled, "Two!"

"Two what?" Howard bellowed.

"Too low," Springstead said. "Much too low."

DON'T UNPACK
YOUR BAGS

The legendary Casey Stengel had many great seasons managing the New York Yankees. He led the Bronx Bombers to seven World Series championships in his 12 seasons with the Yankees.

Over his 25 years as a big league manager, Stengel's name became almost synonymous with success, as he won 1,926 games over that time. But when he took over as the skipper of the crosstown New York Mets in 1962, Stengel saw more bad baseball in a year than he had seen in all his days wearing Yankee pinstripes.

Of his team's escapades, Stengel once said, "There comes a time in every man's life at least once; and I've had plenty of them."

One day shortly after assuming the helm of the Mets, Stengel was asked by New York media about the potential of two of his team's most highly touted prospects, both of whom were 20 years old and in their first attempt to make the major league roster.

"In ten years, Ed Kranepool has a chance to be a star," Stengel replied. "And in ten years, the other guy has a chance to be 30."

HEAVYWEIGHT NEGOTIATOR

Charlie Kerfeld broke into the major leagues with an impressive rookie season in 1986. The relief pitcher posted a record of 11–2 with a 2.59 ERA and seven saves. When he renegotiated his contract with the Houston Astros for the 1987 season, Kerfeld had some rather odd demands in order to close the deal.

The right-handed relief pitcher was fond of his uniform number 37 and wanted to find a way to memorialize that number in his contract. So when the Astros offered him a salary of $110,000 for the season, Kerfeld turned it down, insisting the team pay him $110,037.37. He further demanded the team throw in 37 boxes of Jell-o to complete the agreement. The Astros said yes to both the additional $37.37, and the 37 boxes of Jell-o, and Kerfeld was happy.

He was not thin, however, and within two years, weight problems drove him out of the game at age twenty-four. When Kerfeld was released, many wondered what would have happened had he not insisted on the Jell-o.

BETTER THAN WHEATIES

D oug Rader was one of the National League's premier third basemen in the late 1960s and early '70s, mostly playing for the Houston Astros. Later, Rader managed the Texas Rangers, California Angels, and Chicago White Sox. During his playing days, he was known as a solid power hitter who also had a good glove. He hit 20 or more homers three times and drove in 80 or more runs four times in a five year stretch, while leading the NL's third basemen in fielding percentage and assists twice each.

But Rader was also quirky and known for occasional whacky behavior. Often, teammates would catch him eating baseball cards in the dugout during games. When they asked him why he was munching on the cardboard, Rader replied by saying it was the best and quickest way that he could absorb statistical information of the opposing players.

ONE OF A KIND

Many interesting characters have dotted the landscape of professional sports. Few have expressed their individuality in such unique ways as baseball's Jimmy Piersall. Piersall was an outfielder for the Boston Red Sox, Cleveland Indians, and California Angels in the 1950s and '60s, and was the subject of the movie *Fear Strikes Out*, which detailed his troublesome childhood and subsequent psychological problems. A talented player, Piersall was known more for his moments of unusual behavior.

Once, when teammate Milt Bolling was approaching home plate after hitting a home run, Piersall came out of the dugout to greet Bolling at the plate. Rather than a handshake or pat on the back, Piersall celebrated Bolling's hit by pulling out a water pistol and spraying home plate just before Bolling crossed the plate.

Another time, after being kicked out of a game for arguing with the umpires, Piersall climbed onto the roof of the grandstand and from that perch began to heckle the umpires. He ended up suspended for three games.

On yet another occasion, Piersall went out to his position in center field with a can of bug spray in hand. As the game proceeded, in between pitches, Piersall sprayed a cloud of the poison at the bugs that supposedly hovered around him.

In 1960, while playing for the Indians, Piersall was involved in one of the game's most memorable temper tantrums. The Indians were playing a doubleheader against the Chicago White Sox at Chicago's Comiskey Park. Umpires tossed Piersall out of the first game for arguing. This prompted Piersall to go berserk, littering the field with bats, helmets, gloves, and finally a sand bucket. But he was not finished.

The White Sox had installed a brand-new flashing scoreboard, which was the first of its kind in the American League and the pride of Sox owner Bill Veeck. When the second game ended, Piersall turned and fired an orange and then a baseball at the scoreboard. He said he threw the orange because it hit him in the head as he caught the game's last out. The baseball, he said he threw simply because he didn't like the scoreboard. "I was aiming for the glass but I missed," he later told the media.

During the 1960 season, while in the lineup as the regular centerfielder for the Indians, Piersall went through an odd series of displays in which he played out of position at his own behest.

At Boston's Fenway Park, he walked from his centerfield position and sat down behind the flagpole in the outfield. The following week at Yankee Stadium, he hid himself behind the monuments in the outfield. In his own game of hide-and-seek, he eventually emerged to take his place in center, but positioned himself nearly 100 feet deeper than his normal spot. The game was held up until manager Joe Gordon convinced Piersall to move in. Later in the game, as Piersall trotted out to his position, he stopped just a few feet behind second base and stationed himself there. Gordon and second baseman Ken Aspromonte finally coaxed him to return to his position.

Piersall may have saved his most famous moment for last. As he wound down his career with the Angels in 1966, to commemorate his 100th career home run, Piersall made his way around the bases—from first step out of the batter's box all the way until he crossed home plate— running backwards.

HAVE A NICE STAY

Most aspiring major leaguers dream about the first day they actually make it to the big leagues. What it will feel like to put on the uniform and run out onto a major league field.

For Harry Heitman, that feeling didn't last very long. On July 27, 1918, Heitman was brought to the Brooklyn Dodgers. On that first day, he was to pitch against the St. Louis Cardinals. He had hardly warmed up when his dream came crashing down. Heitman faced just five batters, getting only one out. The other four hitters he faced ripped two triples and two singles before Heitman was removed from the game.

He walked off the mound to the showers with an ERA of 108.00, and he just kept walking, never to return. That very afternoon, Heitman tossed his glove in the trash and enlisted in the Navy.

IT WAS A GREAT MOMENT, BUT I DON'T REMEMBER MUCH

Billy Herman was a fine major league player during the 1930s for the Chicago Cubs. The second baseman played for nearly two decades, made several All-Star teams, and had a lifetime .304 batting average. But the beginning of Herman's career was not exactly considered a memorable one . . . at least for him.

For his big league debut, Herman was in the starting lineup against the Cincinnati Reds and pitcher Si Johnson. Anxious to prove he belonged, Herman dug into the batter's box with steely determination. At Johnson's first pitch, Herman swung so hard that when he foul tipped the ball, it drove down into the ground in back of home plate with such spin on it, that the reverse English caused the ball to bounce straight back up into Herman's head. The force of the ball knocked Herman out cold. Lying at the plate, he had to be carried off on a stretcher. In a rather ignominious beginning to what would turn out to be a great career, Billy Herman had been knocked out by his own foul ball.

WHAT A CARD!

Many players have attempted to play pranks on the trading card companies. Each year, when the card companies send photographers to take pictures of the players, some attempt to sneak something into the shot to have their prank recorded for history. And sometimes, it actually works.

Such was the case in 1969 with a young third baseman for the California Angels. Aurelio Rodriguez became a solid major leaguer for the Angels, Detroit Tigers, and others, but at the time he was a virtual unknown.

Rodriguez's teammates had seen the Topps' photographer searching for Rodriguez, but they could tell the man had no real idea of what the young infielder looked like. So Angels players urged Rodriguez to trick the photographer by switching uniforms with someone else. Rodriguez agreed, and as a result, the Topps photographer shot the wrong person, thinking it was Rodriguez.

When Aurelio Rodriguez's 1969 Topps trading card #653 was released, the person wearing the Angels uniform whose face showed up on the card was actually a 16-year-old Angels batboy named Leonard Garcia.

EXCUSES, EXCUSES

Many a player has attempted to come up with an excuse for sitting out a game in order to take a day off. Two of the more creative excuses around baseball circles still are talked about today.

Jose Cardenal was an outfielder for eight teams from 1963–1980. Cardenal was described as a player who felt if he couldn't give 100 percent effort, it would be better to give no effort at all. Many managers complained that they sometimes had a difficult chore of arguing with Cardenal while he explained to them why he should remain in the comfort of the dugout rather than in the hot sun in right field.

Before one road game in 1972, Cardenal approached Cubs' manager Whitey Lockman and told him he needed to sit out. When Lockman asked why, Cardenal's reply was "Crickets."

The manager told his player he needed further explanation. Cardenal complained that the crickets in his hotel room had made so much noise the night before that he couldn't get to sleep and was too tired to play.

In 1974, he may have topped that explanation when he asked for a couple of days to sit out—because his eyelid was stuck open.

EXCUSES, EXCUSES, II

Perhaps it had something to do with playing outfield for the Cubs—because Chicago had another interesting case before Cardenal.

Lou Novikoff played outfield for the Cubs from 1941–44. His nickname was "The Mad Russian," and it wasn't just because he was of Russian descent.

No matter how far or hard the ball was hit, Novikoff would back up only so far and then no further. Most often, the ball would rebound off the wall and shoot past him back toward the infield.

When frustrated Cubs manager Charlie Grimm asked Novikoff why he constantly gave up on these seemingly catchable balls, Novikoff explained that he had a terrorizing fear of vines. (And if you've ever seen the ivy-covered walls of Wrigley Field, you know this is a problem.)

Grimm tried everything possible to cure his odd outfielder's fear. He brought in poisonous goldenrod to show Novikoff that they were different from the vines in Wrigley. He rubbed the Wrigley vines all over his own face and hands, and even chewed on them, to prove the ivy was not poisonous. But Novikoff never was able to overcome his fear, and balls continued to sail over his head.

THIS SPUD'S FOR YOU

Even the minor leagues have their share of amazing stories. Perhaps the most infamous occurred in 1987 and involved a 25-year-old second string catcher named Dave Bresnahan. Bresnahan played for the Williamsport (Pennsylvania) Bills of the Class-AA Eastern League. The Bills were playing in a meaningless late-season home game at the end of August, and Bresnahan decided to liven things up.

Before the game, Bresnahan had holed up in his locker and spent several minutes peeling and sculpting a potato into the shape of a baseball. Bresnahan knew he would be behind the plate during that day's game, and he waited for the opportune time to put his plan into action. In the fifth inning, he found his opportunity. With a runner on third base, Bresnahan pulled the potato from his back pocket and concealed it in his mitt. When the pitcher threw to the plate, Bresnahan grabbed the potato with his bare hand, caught the pitch, and then threw the potato wildly past his third baseman. Bresnahan was hoping the base runner would think he made an errant pick-off throw, and would head for home. The play worked just as the catcher had planned. The runner at third scampered home, where Bresnahan was waiting with the baseball and tagged him out.

There was ample confusion following the play. While both teams tried to sort out the confusion, an umpire retrieved the potato from the third base line, and recognizing what had happened, awarded the runner home for Bresnahan's deception.

The following day, Bresnahan was fined by his manager and then released by the Bills' parent club, the Cleveland Indians, for actions they considered to be an affront to the integrity of the game.

Although his four-year professional baseball career was over, Bresnahan became an instant celebrity. He fielded numerous interview requests from around the world and was named the 1987 Sports Person of the Year by *Chicago Tribune* columnist Bob Verdi.

In 1988, the Williamsport Bills held a Dave Bresnahan Day, bringing the retired catcher back and retiring his uniform number 59. In addressing the more than 4,000 fans in attendance, Bresnahan told them, "Lou Gehrig had to play in 2,130 consecutive games and hit .340 for his number to be retired, and all I had to do was bat .140 and throw a potato."

The potato was salvaged from a trash can after the game by a teenaged boy and offered to the National Baseball Hall of Fame and Museum in Cooperstown, N.Y. Officials reportedly showed little interest in its acquisition. So baseball's most famous spud now resides in a specimen jar at the Baseball Reliquary. Today, Bresnahan is a stockbroker.

WELCOME
TO THE CIRCUS

Bill Veeck was one of the most imaginative promoters in baseball. Some called him a genius. Others called him eccentric. Either way, he certainly left his mark on the game.

Perhaps the one day that best demonstrated Veeck's Barnumesque ideas was August 18, 1951. Veeck's team, the St. Louis Browns, was dismal. Attendance was down, and Veeck was about to give people reasons to come to the park other than to see his team win. On this day in August, the Browns played a memorable doubleheader against the Detroit Tigers at Sportsman's Park in St. Louis. In taking part in the American League's 50th anniversary celebration, which happened to coincide with the 50th anniversary of the Falstaff Brewing Company, the Browns' radio sponsor, Veeck surprised fans by putting a clown on the field, persuading pitcher Satchel Paige to play the drums in a jazz quartet, and paying a 26-year-old 3'7" 65-lb midget to jump out of a seven-foot birthday cake wearing a miniature Browns uniform and slippers turned up at the ends like an those of an elf.

But Veeck was not done. In the bottom of the first inning of the second game, fans were once again surprised, this time by the announcement of the midget from the cake as a pinch hitter into the ballgame. Over the public address system, the words rang out, "Number one-eighth, Eddie Gaedel, batting for [Frank] Saucier."

Browns manager Zach Taylor actually sent Gaedel to the plate to pinch hit. Tigers manager Red Rolfe immediately protested, but Taylor produced a legitimate contract, filed with the American League and cleared by umpire Ed Hurley.

Gaedel, whose strike zone measured 1 ½ inches, drew a walk on four pitches from amused Tigers' pitcher Bob Cain. Then he ran to first base and was replaced by pinch-runner Jim Delsing. Gaedel received a standing ovation from Browns fans and promptly retired on the spot. His brief Major League career was over just minutes after it had begun.

Fans were hoping to see Gaedel swing his toy-like bat, assuming Cain could get a pitch in his strike zone. But Gaedel was instructed by Veeck not to swing. The owner told his one-day wonder to crouch as low as possible and warned him not to swing. Veeck even warned Gaedel that for good measure a high-powered rifle would be trained upon him from the stands. Gaedel was happy to take a walk and make history as the shortest baseball player ever to appear in a big league game.

In the end, the Browns lost the game 6-2, despite the hoopla. For Gaedel's contribution, he was paid $100. Two days after the game, Gaedel, who had been insured by Veeck for $1 million, was banned from appearing in any more big league games by American League president Will Harridge, who was furious with Veeck's antics and unsuccessfully tried to strike Gaedel's name from the baseball record books. Once again, Veeck had made a mark on the game that would not be forgotten.

LOVE MATCH

Former Pittsburgh Pirates home run king Ralph Kiner was among the greatest players of his era. He led the National League in home runs seven consecutive seasons, from 1946-1952, and was elected into the Baseball Hall of Fame in 1975. But as a baseball announcer, Kiner was known as the master of malapropisms. In fact, his propensity for amazing lines during broadcasts was so renown, his verbal missteps became known as "Kiner-isms." Among his most classic Kinerisms were the following two:

"All of the Mets' road wins against the Dodgers this year have been at Dodger Stadium." And: "The Hall of Fame ceremonies are on the 31st and 32nd of June."

One day during a break in a broadcast, Kiner was telling his broadcasting buddy, Lindsey Nelson, about his wife, the former tennis star Nancy Chaffee.

"When I married Nancy, I vowed I'd beat her at tennis someday," Kiner told Nelson. "After six months, she beat me 6–2. After a year, she beat me 6–4. After we were married a year and a half, I pushed her to 7–5. Then it happened—she had a bad day and I had a good one, and I beat her 17–15."

"Good for you, Ralph," exclaimed Nelson. "Was she sick?"

"Of course not!" Kiner snapped indignantly. "But she was eight months pregnant."

THE PIED PIPER?

Sporting events have seen all types of strange ejections—players from the bench, coaches, grounds crew members, even fans. But the stadium organist?

That's exactly what happened during a minor league baseball game at Jack Russell Stadium in Florida during the 1985 season. The Clearwater Phillies were locked in a tight game, when the stadium organist intervened on the Phillies behalf and was kicked out of the stadium by the umpiring crew.

The organist, Wilbur Snapp, felt the umpires had made a bad call against the Phillies and decided to make his opinion known. He reacted to the call by playing the song "Three Blind Mice." The umpires, on to the not-so-subtle message, immediately ejected Snapp from the stadium.

DIZZY TIZZY

Dizzy Dean was one of the great characters in baseball. His country humor and innocence endeared him to the press and fans alike. Dean was a star pitcher for the St. Louis Cardinals in the 1930s and '40s before heading to the broadcast booth.

Dean was a 30-game winner for the Cards, but is best known for a slew of memorable one-liners.

Once speaking about Negro League pitching great Satchel Paige, Dean said, "If Satch and I were pitching on the same team, we'd cinch the pennant by July 4 and go fishing until World Series time."

Dean didn't pitch with Paige, but for a time, Dean did team up with his brother Paul on the same staff for the St. Louis Cardinals. Once, after Dean had pitched a one-hitter in the first game of a double-header, brother Paul went one better by tossing a no-hitter in the nightcap. Following the game, Dean told the press, "Shucks, if I'd known Paul was gonna pitch a no-hitter, I'd a pitched one, too."

Often, Dean's words rang true. Once, during the close of the 1934 season, Dean had grown leery of the quality of the Cardinals pitching staff beyond himself and Paul. One day, with the World Series looming, Dean was asked how the

Cardinals expected to fare against the Detroit Tigers. "Me and Paul," Dean replied, "will win two games apiece."

While the words may not have seemed like a confidence booster for his teammates, they did prove to be somewhat prophetic. The Cards won games 1, 2, 6, and 7—all games pitched by the brothers, to take the Series 4 games to 3.

Dean also became known for his verbal bloopers. During one game in the 1934 World Series, he was hit on the head by a fly ball. Sometime later, he was asked how he felt. He told the press he was fine and then explained: "The doctors x-rayed my head and found nothing."

Later, as a broadcaster, Dean wrapped up his commentary of a 1–0 game he had called by telling his audience, "The game was closer than the score indicated."

Dean was also accused of serving as a poor role model for students of the English language because of his poor use of grammar and diction. Retorted Dean, "A lot of people who don't say ain't, ain't eatin'!"

Later, during an interview with a British reporter, Dean was asked, "Mr. Dean, don't you know the king's English?"

"Sure, I do," Dean replied after a moment's reflection, "and so is the queen."

TWO-TIMER

D ale Holman was a top minor league player for a handful of teams. The outfielder was the seemingly eternal prospect who always hit well at every level of the minors but was never in the right place to get a shot at the big leagues. He was also at the center of one of the strangest stories in baseball.

On June 30, 1986, Holman was playing for the Syracuse Chiefs, then the AAA affiliate of the Toronto Blue Jays. The Chiefs were taking on the Richmond Braves, the AAA affiliate of the Atlanta Braves, in an International League game.

During the game, Holman came to bat with two on and promptly laced a double, scoring both runners and giving Syracuse a brief lead. A short time later, the game was suspended, to be completed at a later date. All statistics and records from the game would be kept and merely added to once the remainder of the game was played out. Following the game, Holman was released by the Chiefs, only to be signed by Richmond.

Several days later, when the suspended game was scheduled to be completed, Holman was in the lineup in the outfield for the Braves, as a substitute for a player who had originally started the game when it was first played.

Holman singled and doubled in his two trips to the plate for the Braves that night, as the suspended game was completed. When the box score was compiled from the game, it showed that very rare statistical oddity—that Dale Holman had collected a hit for two opposing teams in the same game!

HELLO AGAIN

A s the 1987 Major League Baseball season wore down, several teams in the pennant chase jockeyed to make key trades that could help them overcome their competition. A key pinch hitter, another arm in the bullpen, or a late-inning defensive replacement could help teams get to the top.

Right-handed relief pitcher Dickie Noles was one player many teams attempted to pry away from the Chicago Cubs. Late in the season, the Detroit Tigers swung a deal to bring Noles to the Motor City. In return, the Cubs would receive a player to be named later from the Tigers. Noles pitched in just four games for the Tigers, and Detroit didn't make it to the postseason.

When the season was over, management for the Tigers and Cubs got together to discuss completing the trade and determining the player to be named. When they had finished the discussion, it was decided that Noles would be that player. So, Noles reported back to the Cubs.

What it all meant was that in the course of just a few weeks, Dickie Noles became the first player in baseball history to be traded for himself.

ASTONISHING ALL-TIME BASEBALL TEAMS

ALL-FINANCIAL BASEBALL TEAM

C	Jim Price
1B	Norm Cash
2B	Chuck Schilling
SS	Ernie Banks
3B	Don Money
OF	Barry Bonds
OF	Reid Nichols
OF	Oscar Gamble
P	Felipe Lira
P	Wes Stock
P	Brad Penny

ALL-BUILDERS BASEBALL TEAM

C	Phil Roof
1B	Mickey Mantle
2B	Jay Bell
SS	Andy Sheets
3B	Jim Davenport
OF	Matt Stairs
OF	Rowland Office
OF	Don Lock
OF	Terry Puhl
P	Jimmy Key
P	Dennis Lamp
P	John Rocker
P	Tom House
P	Stan Wall
P	Dick Pole

ALL-ROMANCE BASEBALL TEAM

C	Rick Sweet
1B	Paul Casanova
2B	Pete Rose
SS	Bobby Valentine
3B	Jim Ray Hart
OF	Cupid Childs
OF	Ellis Valentine
OF	Sandy Amoros
DH	Beau Bell
UTIL	Jimmy Ring
P	Steve Sparks
P	Ron Darling
P	Rich Batchelor

ALL-LAW-AND-ORDER BASEBALL TEAM

C	Johnny Bench
1B	Joe Judge
2B	Tom Lawless
SS	Craig Counsell
3B	Vance Law
OF	Dave Justice
OF	Walt Bond
OF	Willie Miranda
DH	Lee Bales
P	Vern Law
P	George Case

ALL-FIELD-AND-STREAM BASEBALL TEAM

C	Randy Bobb	DH	Jess Pike
1B	Randy Bass	P	Steve Trout
2B	Gus Gil	P	Randy Wolf
SS	Chico Salmon	P	George Haddock
3B	Bobby Sturgeon	P	Bob Moose
INF	Andy Fox	P	Joel Finch
INF	Robin Yount	P	Craig Swan
INF	Doug Griffin	P	Mike Parrott
OF	Tim Salmon	P	Clay Roe
OF	Kevin Bass	P	Bob Cluck
OF	Aaron Pointer	P	Doug Bird
OF	Kevin Flora		
OF	Sammy Drake		
OF	Jayhawk Owens		

ALL-ANATOMY BASEBALL TEAM

C	Barry Foote
1B	Harry Cheek
2B	Dave Brain
SS	Greg Legg
3B	Jim Hart
OF	Bob Pate
OF	Mike Palm
OF	Ed Head
P	Bill Hands
P	Rich Hand
P	Roy Face
P	Rollie Fingers
P	Ricky Bones
P	Bartolo Colon
P	Mike Overy
P	Don Gullett
P	Dave Beard
P	Scott Brow

ALL-TERRAIN BASEBALL TEAM

C	Steve Lake
1B	Dave Valle
2B	Gary Woods
SS	Gene Alley
3B	Brook Jacoby
OF	Mickey Rivers
OF	Tom Marsh
OF	Louie Meadows
OF	Ron Stone
DH	Ruben Sierra
PH	Dusty Rhodes
P	Chan Ho Park
P	Jose Mesa
P	Doug Creek
P	Lee Tunnell
P	Luis Arroyo
P	Matt Beech
P	Ken Hill
P	John Wetteland

ALL-FOOD BASEBALL TEAM

C	Johnny Oates
1B	Johnny Romano
2B	Gene Leek
SS	Bobby Wine
3B	Chet Lemon
OF	Zach Wheat
OF	Billy Bean
OF	Jim Rice
OF	Darryl Strawberry
OF	Ginger Beaumont
DH	Duke Carmel
P	Bob Veale
P	David Cone
P	Pete Hamm
P	Mark Lemongello
P	Terry Cornutt
P	Steve Curry
P	Steve Gerkin
P	Bob Lemon
P	Jose Lima
MGR	Herman Franks & Mayo Smith

ALL-RELIGION BASEBALL TEAM

C	Steve Christmas
1B	Jim Gentile
2B	Lave Cross
SS	Johnny Temple
3B	Max Bishop
OF	John Moses
OF	Angel Mangual
OF	Bob Christian
OF	Von Joshua
OF	Larry Parrish
OF	Luke Easter
OF	Johnny Priest
OF	Howie Nunn
OF	Billy Sunday
DH	Bris Lord
P	Eddie Solomon
P	Adrian Devine
P	Preacher Roe
P	Bill Parsons
P	Amos Russie
P	Micah Bowie

ALL-INTERNATIONAL BASEBALL TEAM

C   Jim French

1B   Joe Hague

2B   Jeff Kent

SS   Miguel Cairo

3B   Kelly Paris

OF   Clyde Milan

OF   Steve Gibralter

OF   Trenidad Hubbard

OF   Bill Roman

DH   Tim Ireland

P   Jim Britton

P   Paul Moskau

P   Israel Sanchez

P   Mark Portugal

P   Andrew Lorraine

P   Alex Madrid

ASTONISHING BUT TRUE
BASEBALL TRIVIA

Former Detroit Tigers outfielder Willie Horton
was the youngest of 21 children.

Rod Carew is the only Hall of Famer born on a train.

Babe Ruth once led the American League
in earned run average as a pitcher in 1916,
going 23–13 with a 1.75 ERA.

Hall of Fame pitcher Hoyt Wilhelm fought in
the Battle of the Bulge in WWII, suffering wounds
that led to a permanently crooked neck.

The 1962 New York Mets had teammates named
Bob Miller. They were both pitchers and roommates!

The 1991–92 San Francisco Giants had many games when their starting battery (pitcher & catcher) was Black (Bud) & Decker (Steve).

Former catcher Moe Berg was a spy during WWII.

Ken Griffey Jr. and Stan Musial not only hail from the same birthplace—Donora, Pa., but they also share the same birthday—November 21.

Indians shortstop Lou Boudreau, who was the 1948 A.L. MVP, was the father-in-law of the 1968 A.L. MVP, Denny McLain.

Randy Moffitt, who pitched for the Giants, Astros, and Blue Jays (1972–83) was the brother of tennis great Billie Jean King.

Four baseball Hall of Famers once played basketball for the Harlem Globetrotters—Bob Gibson, Ferguson Jenkins, Lou Brock, and Satchel Paige.

In a game between the Cincinnati Reds and Chicago Cubs on June 29, 1913, only one baseball was used for the entire nine-inning game.

Former teammates Fernando Valenzuela and Dave Stewart both threw no-hitters on the same day, June 30, 1990. Valenzuela's came for the Dodgers, Stewart's for the A's.

00 was the uniform number worn by pitcher Omar Oliveras to reflect his initials.

Outfielder Chad Curtis married his wife,
Candace, on May 7, 1990, at the courthouse
in Davenport, Iowa, while wearing his
Quad Cities Angels uniform, at 1:30 p.m.,
prior to his 2 p.m. minor league game.

The game was called "base ball" until the 1930s.

The sign at the town border of Pierson, Fla.,
reads: *Fern capital of the world and hometown
of Chipper Jones*. Schools have been named for
former major leaguers: Jackie Robinson, Roberto
Clemente, Walter Johnson, Gil Hodges, Jim Thorpe,
Steve Garvey, and Tim McCarver.

The 1911 Yankees held spring training in Bermuda.

The initials of former Red Sox owners
Thomas A. Yawkey and wife Jean R. Yawkey,
TAY and JRY, appear in Morse code on
the Fenway Park scoreboard.

$\frac{1}{8}$ was the uniform number worn by
3'7", 65-pound Eddie Gaedel during a pinch
hit appearance for the St. Louis Browns in 1951.

Joel Youngblood had hits for two different teams
on the same day, August 14, 1982. He had a hit
for the Mets in a day game, was traded to Montreal
during the game, flew to meet his new team for
their game that night, and got a hit for the Expos.

Immediately after recording his 3000th hit
on September 30, 1992, Hall of Famer
George Brett was picked off first base by
Angels pitcher, Tim Fortugno.

In 1948, the Brooklyn Dodgers needed an
announcer, and they liked Ernie Harwell, who
was broadcasting games for the minor league
Atlanta Crackers. The Crackers needed a catcher,
so the two teams made a deal. The Dodgers
traded catcher Cliff Dapper to Atlanta
for announcer Harwell.

Pitcher John Franco of the Mets was ejected from the game on "John Franco Day," May 11, 1996.

On July 21, 1970, San Diego Padres manager Preston Gomez removed pitcher Clay Kirby from a tie game for a pinch hitter in the bottom of the eighth, even though Kirby was three outs away from completing a no-hitter.

In 1998, the Independent League Pacific Suns traded pitcher Ken Krahenbuhl to the Greenville (Mississippi) Bluesmen for a player to be named, cash, and 10 pounds of Mississippi catfish.

Former outfielder Carlos May was the only player in sports history to wear his birthday on the back of his uniform jersey. May who was born on May 17, wore uniform number 17 under his name stitched across the back of his jersey.

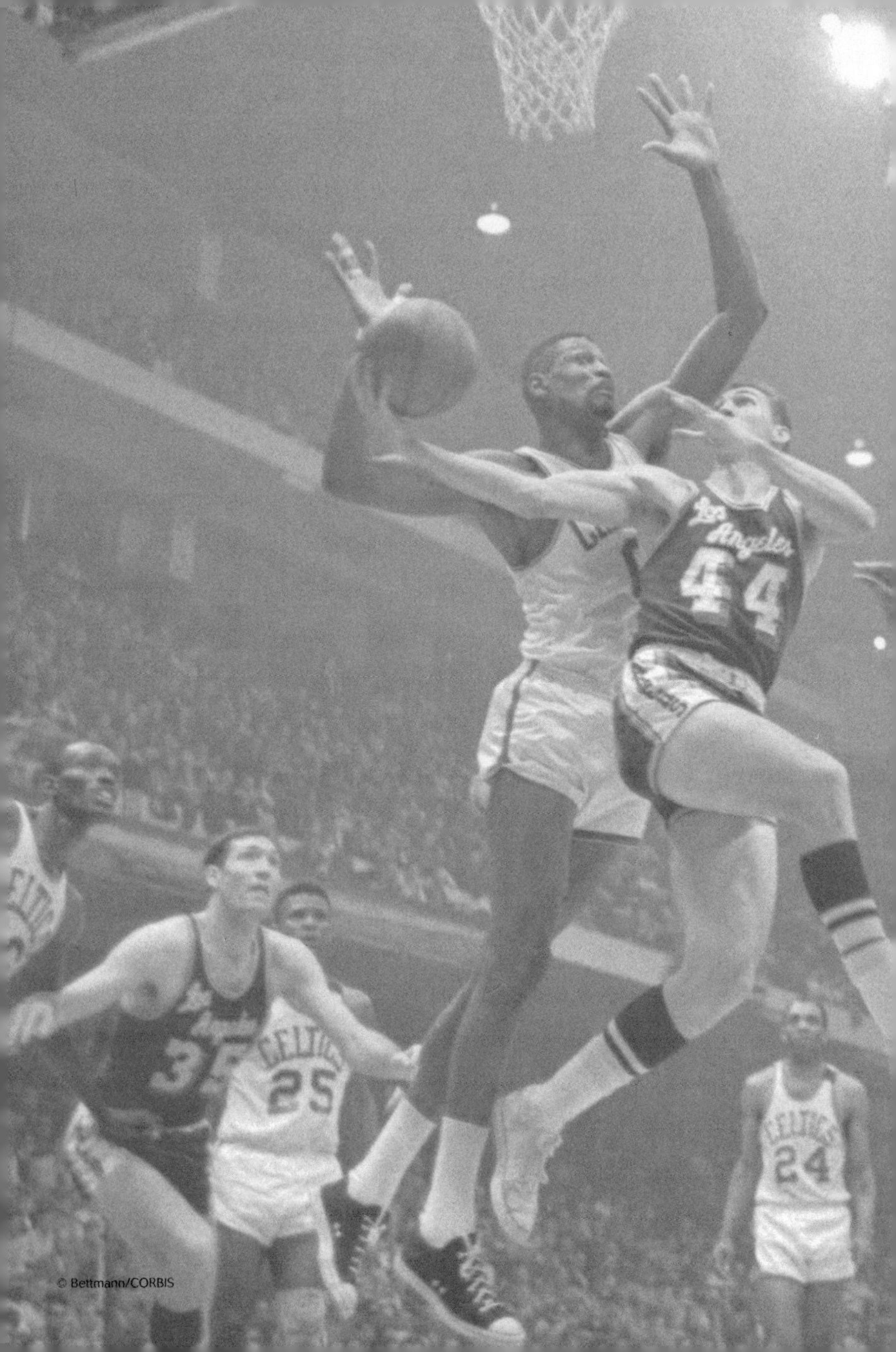
Los Angeles
44
Los Angeles
35
CELTICS
25
CELTICS
24

ASTONISHING BUT TRUE BASKETBALL STORIES

SO YOU WANT
TO BE A REFEREE?

Veteran basketball officials Cliff Ogden and Alex George learned firsthand just how difficult the job of a referee can be. The year was 1956, and Ogden and George were officiating a game between the University of Wichita and the University of Detroit, being played on Wichita's home court, which was known in those days for hosting crowds that were normally unruly and often inebriated.

Detroit was down by one point with four seconds to play, as they began to inbound the ball. They pushed the ball into the frontcourt, and before time ran out, a Detroit player was able to get off a shot. As Ogden and George both followed the arc of the ball toward the hoop, they were shocked to see that a Wichita fan had tossed an overcoat from the field house balcony and landed it right over the rim. The ball hit the coat and bounced off as the buzzer sounded.

Ogden and George were faced with a situation they had never encountered before. As they contemplated what call to make, they were surrounded by a wild mob of Wichita fans who were scrambling across the court, celebrating.

George turned to Ogden and said, "It's a hundred and twenty feet to our dressing room, and I'm not going to call it anything until we both get to the door."

With the door locked behind the two officials, George notified both teams that he had called the shot good, and the basket gave Detroit a one-point win.

Wisely, Ogden and George waited until they could hear no fans remaining in the Wichita field house before leaving their dressing room and heading home. It was a situation they hoped they would never face again.

BAD HAIR DAY

In 1983, Utah Jazz guard Jerry Eaves was killing time on the road prior to a big game against the Phoenix Suns. Eaves found a local Phoenix shop to get his hair cut. Unfortunately for Eaves, it was a day at the salon gone awry. He was quite disappointed and somewhat embarrassed when he saw the results. A large bald spot was apparent atop Eaves' head, left by the barber's handiwork. Distraught, Eaves gathered a clump of hair that had been cut from his head, took it with him and used an adhesive to stick the clump of cut hair to the bald spot.

During the game that evening, as Eaves was running down the court in the second quarter, the clump of hair fell out and landed on the court. Eaves reached down, grabbed the hair and stuffed it in his pants. Eaves then took himself out of the game and headed for the locker room, where he borrowed a car from the team's director of broadcasting, Dave Fredman, and drove back to the team hotel, where he glued the hair clump back into place over the bald spot. Once the hair was back in place, Eaves returned to the arena for the game.

The hair clump stayed in place for the entire second half, but by game's end, Eaves had acquired a new nickname that also stuck. Team broadcaster Rod Hundley immediately began calling Eaves "Razor," which became his new moniker around the league.

ONE ON FIVE

In 1972, the West Coast Christian College Knights were taking on the University of California at Santa Cruz in a basketball game, when they found themselves in serious foul trouble.

With just over two minutes left in the game, the Knights led the Sea Lions of Santa Cruz by the score of 70–57. But how the Knights would hold that lead was the question on everyone's mind in attendance that day.

Every player on the WCCC team had fouled out, with the exception of guard Mike Lockhart, and he had four fouls—one away from disqualification.

"We started the game in a tandem zone," Lockhart explained of his team's defensive plans following the game. "Then we went to a straight two-three zone. After we were down to four guys we used a two-two box. Then [with three players] a one-two diamond. Then [with two players] a one-one zone. Finally a one."

Incredibly, Lockhart was only outscored 10–5 by the five Santa Cruz players during the game's final two minutes, and he single-handedly held on to see the Knights win the game 75–67.

SHORT STOP?

Bill Sharman was a part of one of the finest backcourt tandems in NBA history. In the 1950s, Sharman teamed with Bob Cousy to help lead the Boston Celtics to four NBA championships. One of the greatest free throw shooters ever, Sharman hit 88.3% of his shots from the charity stripe over his career and led the league in free throw percentage a record seven times. He was elected to the Pro Basketball Hall of Fame in 1975. Sharman also coached the Los Angeles Lakers to an NBA title in 1972, a season in which his team won a league-record 33 consecutive games.

What most people don't remember about Sharman, however, is that he also played baseball, making it to the major leagues. His stay in the big leagues was one of the shortest and oddest ever known.

Late in the 1951 season, the Brooklyn Dodgers called Sharman up to be with the team during the pennant race. Sharman rode the bench as the Dodgers blew a huge lead in the final month and never got into a game. On September 27, the Dodgers were involved in a tense game, and emotions were a bit raw. Several players took exception to some calls made by umpire Frank Dascoli and began to make their displeasure known from the bench.

Dascoli was not happy. After a warning to the Dodgers bench, the razzing continued, so Dascoli decided to throw the entire Brooklyn bench out of the game. Every player, including Sharman, was ordered to leave the dugout. Thus, Bill Sharman became the only player in baseball history to be thrown out of a big league game without having played in one.

DEE-FENSE!

The most amazing basketball game of all time must also have been the most difficult to watch.

In 1925, Kensal High and Pingree High, two Fargo, N. Dak., girls high school teams, were locked in a defensive struggle. They played to a scoreless tie at the end of regulation time.

After three overtime periods that followed, the teams were still deadlocked at 0–0. It was determined that the best next step was to not have the girls take the court again, but rather to decide the contest by flipping a coin. While the referee flipped a quarter, Kensal's weary coach correctly called heads, and Pingree wound up a 0–0 loser.

ASTONISHING ALL-TIME BASKETBALL TEAMS

ALL-WALL-STREET BASKETBALL TEAM

G   Phil Bond
G   Mark Price
C   Laron Profit
F   Eric Money
F   Gene Banks

ALL-GEOGRAPHY BASKETBALL TEAM

G   Brad Holland
G   Michael Jordan
C   Mike Brittain
F   Ken Spain
F   Kendall Rhine

ALL-NAVY BASKETBALL TEAM

G   Darrell Carrier
G   John Battle
C   Charlie Shipp
F   Terry Furlow
F   Kenny Sailors

ALL-BOATING BASKETBALL TEAM

G   Danny Ferry
G   Matt Finn
C   Eddie Mast
F   Curtis Rowe
F   Louis Orr

ALL-STAR-SPANGLED BASKETBALL TEAM

G   World B. Free
G   Claude English
C   George Washington
F   Marcus Liberty
F   Keith Starr

ALL-THE-PRESIDENT'S-MEN BASKETBALL TEAM

G   Norm Nixon
G   Earl Monroe
C   George Washington
F   Gene Kennedy
F   Garfield Heard

ALL-THE-PRESIDENT'S-MEN BASKETBALL TEAM II

G   TJ Ford
G   Gary Grant
C   Roosevelt Bowie
F   Vince Carter
F   Richard Jefferson

ALL-SECOND-CAREER BASKETBALL TEAM

G   Bill Bradley (Senator, New York)
G   Chuck Connors ("The Rifleman")
C   Tom McMillan (Congressman, Maryland)
F   Wayman Tisdale (Jazz Musician)
F   Mark Hendrickson (Major League Baseball Player)

ASTONISHING BUT TRUE FOOTBALL STORIES

TAKING THE FIFTH

F ootball referees are rarely considered to be generous. But during a tight college football game, one popular ref was accidentally more accommodating than he would have liked.

Red Friesell was one of the most respected referees in college football. So it came as a surprise when he was at the center of controversy. It was during a game between Cornell and Dartmouth on November 18, 1940. The field was slick and muddy from late fall rains that had hit Hanover, N.H., Dartmouth's home. Cornell, an Eastern football power at the time, was on the short end of a 3–0 score. It looked as though they were about to be upset, as the clock wound down. Still, the Big Red mounted one last strong drive, moving down the field all the way to the Dartmouth six-yard-line. There, the Mean Green defense prepared for one last stand. Cornell ran three consecutive running plays to move the ball to the one-yard-line. They were then penalized for attempting to call a time-out when they did not have one. Friesell moved the ball back to the six. On fourth down, Cornell attempted a pass, which fell incomplete. But after retrieving the ball, Friesell reset the line of scrimmage at the six-yard-line once again. No one noticed Cornell had already run out of downs, so the two teams lined up for play, with Cornell still on offense. After the snap, Cornell again attempted a pass, and this one was completed, for a fifth down touchdown on the game's final play. The Red won the game 7–3.

With the excitement at the finish, Friesell's error was not noticed. However, shortly after the game ended, players, press, and fans all agreed that Cornell had been given an extra down and the winning points should not count.

Friesell was disheartened after the game, telling the press that he "blew it." In his official report, he accepted responsibility for the error and absolved the other three officials from any blame.

Cornell's response was equally demonstrative of their character. They returned the victory to Dartmouth, which brought to an end Cornell's 18-game winning streak.

Ivy League Commissioner Asa Bushnell put the finishing touches on one of the most amazing finishes to a college football game, when in a telegram to Friesell, he mused, "Don't let it get you down, down, down, down, down."

TRASH TALK

Tim Wrightman was an All-American tight end at UCLA who was drafted by the Chicago Bears in 1985. Wrightman, now an actor, remembers his rookie year in the National Football League and how a wily veteran tried to get the best of him.

The Bears were playing the Super Bowl-contending New York Giants, which meant Wrightman would spend much of the game lined up against superstar linebacker Lawrence Taylor. The rookie knew he would have his hands full attempting to block the fiercest pass rusher in the game. He studied film and carefully reviewed all of his assignments for each play. He wanted to be prepared for this enormous test of his ability to compete at the NFL level. Wrightman had also been apprised of Taylor's infamous prowess to talk, all game long, to his opponents in an effort to wear them down emotionally. Few talked more trash than L.T., so Wrightman made sure he was ready for the verbal barrage.

Early in the game, Taylor looked Wrightman in the eye and said, "Son, I'm going through you on the left; don't hurt yourself trying to stop me."

Wrightman, refusing to be intimidated, shot back, "Sir, is that your left or mine?"

The question froze Taylor long enough to allow Wrightman the chance to put a perfect block on Taylor and allow for a successful Bears offensive play.

Taylor was none too happy, but the rookie had one-upped him.

WRONG-WAY ROY

The Rose Bowl is known as the "granddaddy" of all bowl games. It has been the scene of some of college football's greatest individual performances, amazing plays, and historic finishes. One play stands above the rest among those that will never be forgotten in the lore of college football. It occurred at the 1929 Rose Bowl game between the University of California at Berkley and Georgia Tech, and it was one of the most spectacular and most heartbreaking runs in football history.

In that day, the Rose Bowl was the only postseason college football game. Millions of football fans around the country listened to the game by radio; every major city's newspaper covered the action; and in the aftermath, football fans across the country talked about the game. On the afternoon of Jan. 1, 1929, and for days thereafter, California's Roy Riegels was the most talked-about athlete in America. But it was not exactly the kind of recognition the young man wanted.

Early in the second quarter with the score 0–0, Tech had the ball on its own 20. Tech halfback Stumpy Thomason took the snap and swung wide to his left behind good blocking. Near the 30-yard line, he was hit by two California tacklers. The football squirted out of Thomason's hands and bounced along the grass on the ground of the storied stadium in Pasadena, Calif.

California junior Roy Riegels, who was playing roving center on defense, was in position to make the play. "As the ball fell away from Thomason, I picked it up and ran," Riegels later remembered. "The defense could do that in those days. I started in the right direction but made a complete horseshoe turn after going four or five yards when I saw two players coming at me from the right. In pivoting to get away, I completely lost my bearings. I wasn't out of my head at all. I hadn't been hurt. I just headed the wrong way."

As Riegels galloped downfield, unknowingly headed toward scoring a touchdown for the opponent, alert teammate Benny Lom, a halfback for the Golden Bears, was the first man to react. Lom chased Riegels the length of the field. As Lom gained on Riegels, he shouted frantically, "Stop! Stop! You're going to wrong way!"

At first, the noise of the crowd drowned out Lom's voice. But Riegels later said he knew Lom was chasing him and thought his teammate wanted the ball so he could score the touchdown.

"As I neared the goal line, I could hear Benny yelling for me to throw him the ball. Shucks, I wasn't going to throw it to him after that run," Riegels admitted. "There was nothing going through my mind except that I wanted to make a touchdown. I can't even think of a decent alibi. I just bounced out with the ball, saw a pair of goalposts, and headed for them."

Lom finally caught up to Riegels, grabbed his hand, and spun him around. But by this time, the two men were standing on the one-yard line. As the two men looked upfield at the distant Tech goal line, Riegels realized something was terribly wrong. But before he could make the slightest move, Tech end Frank Waddey plowed into him. Then a wave of Tech players rolled over him, driving him into the end zone as Lom stepped aside.

Referee Herb Dana ruled the ball dead on the one-yard line.

Teammates tried to console Riegels, who sat on the ground for some time holding his head. Even some Georgia Tech players patted him on the shoulders. California coach, Nibs Price had compassion on his player and left Riegels in the game.

On the ensuing play, with California now having the ball with a first down on their own one yard line, Riegels centered the ball accurately to punter Lom. But Tech tackle Vance Maree leaped to block the kick. In the ensuing scramble, California halfback Stan Barr was the last to touch the ball before it bounced out of the end zone. Tech was awarded a safety to lead the game 2–0, and those points proved decisive in the game.

Tech added a touchdown in the third quarter but missed the extra point. California scored in the final two minutes but

would score no more. When the game ended 8–7, Riegels was marked for life. He came to be forever known as "Wrong Way Riegels."

Even though Riegels was elected team captain the following season and made some All-America teams, the moniker stuck. Sponsorship offers came in for upside down cakes, backward walkathons, ties with stripes going the wrong way, and a number of other items.

Under the weight of humiliation that could have crushed him, Riegels turned his place in history into a position of responsibility. The man whose coach once called him "the smartest boy on the squad" was also able to laugh at himself throughout his life and learned to enjoy his infamy.

"Sometimes," he once said, "even my 10-year-old son calls me Wrong Way Riegels."

TWELFTH MAN

Sometimes a college athlete's excitement and intensity just get the best of him. When it happens on a national stage, however, rarely will that athlete cease to hear about his exploit. Such is the case with Alabama football player Tommy Lewis.

In the 1954 Cotton Bowl, the Crimson Tide of Alabama was taking on the mighty Rice Owls in a game that would be remembered more for one play than even the final outcome.

During the game's first quarter, Rice halfback Dicky Maegle took a handoff and sprinted down the right sideline, in front of the Alabama bench on his way to a 95-yard touchdown run, when Lewis, an Alabama fullback, made a play that will long be remembered in football annals.

Standing on the sideline, Lewis watched as Maegle avoided one 'Bama tackler after another and then saw the Rice standout break into the clear with no defender left. As his adrenaline rushed, Lewis reacted. With Maegle 57 yards into his run, Lewis jumped off the sideline and tackled Maegle. Maegle, not expecting the hit, went down in a heap. Lewis, himself so stunned at what he had done, scrambled quickly back to the Alabama bench and tried to look like nothing had happened.

"I kept telling myself, 'I didn't do it. I didn't do it,'" he later said. "But I knew I did."

It was a play the seventy-five thousand spectators and live national television audience had never seen before; nor had the officials, who awarded an automatic touchdown to Maegle.

Lewis told reporters afterward that his reaction came about because he was just "too full of Alabama." While no one ever blamed Lewis for Alabama's 28–6 loss in the game, his feelings of guilt were so deep, that he apologized to Maegle after the game and cried openly in the locker room, saying, "I don't think I'll ever get over it. I know I'm going to hear about this for the rest of my life."

Lewis was right. Maegle turned in the greatest single performance in the history of the Cotton Bowl with 261 yards rushing on only 11 carries and three touchdowns, yet the focus of the game from coast to coast was Lewis's tackle.

Following the game, Ed Sullivan invited Lewis and Maegle to appear live on *The Ed Sullivan Show*. But when he ran short on time, Sullivan wound up only interviewing Lewis and never said a word to Maegle. It seemed that Lewis had become a sort of hero for being so inspired by team spirit that led to his memorable tackle.

Sullivan apologized to Maegle and invited him back to the show to appear by himself. But the slighted halfback declined, saying he was too busy studying for exams.

In spite of Lewis's fame through his bonehead play, he always felt haunted by the incident. Many years after the game, he wrote to Maegle to ask for advice on how to live with his infamy. Maegle wrote back that Lewis should try to see the humor in the situation. But Lewis found it difficult to do so. He would never again watch a Cotton Bowl when Alabama played, for fear of seeing his personal nightmare replayed.

ANSWER?

Steve Spurrier is known as one of the most innovative coaches in all of football. He has won at every level of coaching and has fashioned some of the most prolific offenses the game has ever seen. Spurrier has been known as a bit of a perfectionist who demands much from his players.

Perhaps that mindset comes as a result of his experiences as an NFL player in the 1970s. Spurrier was the quarterback for the hapless 1976 Tampa Bay Buccaneers, which became the first team in NFL history to lose every game of the regular season, finishing at 0–14.

The futility the Bucs experienced in the early years became a breeding ground for success, as just three years after setting the league standard for futility, Tampa Bay made it to the NFC Conference Championship Game.

Still, a number of moments from '76 have made many a blooper reel. Dropped passes, fumbles, missed tackles, and kicks that went awry, the Bucs were a comedy of errors— both on the field and in the locker room. The coach of the Bucs was noted quipster John McKay, who had won college national championships at USC before taking the job in Tampa. McKay's one-liners were well documented by the

beat writers who covered the '76 team and are still fondly remembered. They also made an impact on Bucs' players such as Spurrier.

"I remember a speech McKay was giving us at one point in the season," Spurrier recalled. "He was emphasizing that games were lost in the trenches by failing to block and tackle on the front lines.

"And as he was talking, he noticed a lineman asleep in the back. He called his name, woke him up, and asked, 'Where are most games lost?' And the lineman said, 'Right here in Tampa, sir.'"

HEAD BANGER

During a nationally televised Monday Night Football game, the game's most devastating blow was delivered by none other than a quarterback. Unfortunately, he was also the recipient of that blow.

In 1997, Gus Frerotte was quarterbacking the Washington Redskins as they took on the New York Giants. The 'Skins were underdogs, and their offense, with Frerotte at the helm, had come under fire from the media in recent weeks.

With 2:16 left in the first half, Frerotte went back to pass. A good push from the defensive line forced Frerotte to scramble out of the pocket. After escaping Giants defensive end Bernard Holsey, he found an open lane to the goal line and sprinted into the end zone to give the Redskins a 7–0 lead.

Frerotte was so excited about scoring, he celebrated by firing the football at the wall behind the end zone. Not yet done, when he reached that wall, Frerotte further celebrated by lowering the top of his helmet and head-butting the wall. Unfortunately, the wall was immobile, and Frerotte got the worst of the encounter. He recoiled in pain, fell to the ground, and signaled for immediate medical attention from the sideline.

After being treated, Frerotte returned for one series at the end of the half, then didn't return from the locker room at halftime. He was taken to a hospital for examination, then later returned to the stadium, where he watched the remainder of the game from the locker room.

As the national TV audience endured what would end in a 7–7 tie, they learned that Frerotte had knocked himself out of the game and sustained a concussion that would sideline him for a few weeks. It was clearly one of the NFL's more embarrassing moments.

"It was stupid, but I was fired up," Frerotte said of his escapade. "Things weren't going well, then I get a big play like that."

Redskins head coach Norv Turner said wryly following the game: "I never thought to tell a guy not to do that."

THE DAY THE
SCOUTS SLEPT IN

In 1946, the Washington Redskins used their No. 1 pick in the draft to select back Cal Rossi out of UCLA. Unfortunately, Redskins officials failed to realize that Rossi had only completed his junior year and was thus ineligible to be drafted.

But the Redskins were determined to get their man, so they waited until the next year, hoping to draft Rossi again. In 1947, when the 'Skins first-round choice came up, they once again chose Rossi. Once again, team officials must not have done their homework, because Rossi had earlier declared that he had no intention of playing professional football.

When Rossi lived up to his vow, the Redskins were again deprived of their No. 1 pick, amazingly by choosing the same player two years in a row! It was an unprecedented occurrence for any NFL team before or since.

NOW YOU SEE IT, NOW YOU DON'T

1,000 yards rushing in a single season is the magic mark for all running backs. It is the accepted standard for true success rushing the ball, and those who reach that plateau are in elite company.

In the 1972 season, Dave Hampton had an opportunity to reach that milestone in the Atlanta Falcons' season finale against the Kansas City Chiefs. Late in the fourth quarter, a six-yard run put Hampton over the 1,000 yard mark. The game was temporarily stopped, while Hampton was presented the game ball in a brief ceremony, during which Falcons fans cheered wildly for the first 1,000 yard rusher in franchise history.

To the dismay of the fans—and Hampton himself—his achievement lasted but a few moments. A few plays later, Hampton took a handoff and was dropped for a six-yard loss. Game circumstances led to Hampton getting the ball just one more time, on a play which netted just a one-yard gain. As the clock ran out on the game, and on the Falcons season, Hampton was left with the empty feeling that he had been a 1,000 yard rusher for only a brief time. His season ended with a total of 995 yards.

BULLETIN BOARD
MATERIAL

Before taking his passing game mastery to the NFL, coach Steve Spurrier became one of college football's most successful coaches while at the helm of the University of Florida. Under Spurrier, the Gators won a national title and were consistently among the country's top ten teams.

But Spurrier was known to rile his opponents on more than one occasion by his choice of words that became somewhat inflammatory. Two of the old ball coach's most famous remarks came at the expense of vaunted rivals.

One year during off-season travels throughout the state of Florida in speaking to Gator booster clubs, Spurrier chose to take a poke at Florida State. The Seminoles had recently learned that a Tallahassee shoe store had given members of the FSU team free shoes, which was a violation of NCAA rules. Spurrier couldn't resist the opportunity to rub it in a bit. He told Gator boosters how he was making plans for the coming season and had strategies in place to defeat FSU, or "Free Shoes University." As expected, the boosters roared with approval.

But perhaps Spurrier's most famous comments came in discussing an upcoming game with sectional rival Auburn University. Spurrier informed Gator fans that tragically 20 books had been destroyed in a fire at Auburn's football dormitory.

"But the real tragedy," he declared, "was that fifteen hadn't been colored in yet!"

ASTONISHING ALL-TIME FOOTBALL TEAMS

ALL-GEOGRAPHY FOOTBALL TEAM

Keith Lincoln
Ken Houston
Joe Montana
Warren Moon
Doug France
Tom London
Bubba Paris
Yale Lary
Doug English
Russell Maryland
Robert Brazile
Jerry Rhome
David Boston

ALL-COLOR FOOTBALL TEAM

Joe Lavender
Joe Greene
Luther Blue
Mike Black
Stan White
Joe Rose
Ernie Green
Glenn Redd
Willie Brown
Doyle Orange
Lovell Pinkney

ASTONISHING-BUT-TRUE FOOTBALL TRIVIA

Helmets were not mandatory in pro football until 1944.

Pete Gogolak became the NFL's first soccer-style place kicker in 1964.

In 1978, New York Giants fans were so distraught over their team's poor play that they gathered in the parking lot after a Sunday afternoon game and built a bonfire with their season tickets.

In 1980, NBC experimented by televising the New York Jets-Miami Dolphins game without any announcers. The broadcast used all sound from the field and from the stadium's public address system only.

In 1997, Dan Turk became the punt snapper
for the Washington Redskins. The punter he snapped
the ball to was his brother Matt. Dan also served as
Matt's agent off the field.

The Baltimore Colts found future Hall of Fame
quarterback Johnny Unitas playing semipro football
for the Bluefield Rams in 1955, after he had been
cut by the Pittsburgh Steelers.

In 1962, the Buffalo Bills claimed a San Diego Chargers
quarterback on waivers for $100, to become their starter.
This man later led the Bills to AFL Championship wins
over the Chargers in 1964 and '65. His name: Jack Kemp.

The only kicker ever to be named NFL MVP is Mark
Moseley of the Washington Redskins, in 1982.

Marlin Briscoe became the first African-American
to become a starting quarterback, playing for the
Denver Broncos in 1968.

Two current NFL teams were named for real people—one
for a football man, the other for a historical figure—they
are the Cleveland Browns for Paul Brown and the
Buffalo Bills for "Buffalo Bill" Cody.

Fred Arbanas, tight end of the Kansas City Chiefs from
1962–70, played part of his career with a glass eye,
following a serious eye injury.

Cleveland quarterback Otto Graham played
in the championship game in each of his
10 seasons in pro football.

In 1994, Miami's Don Shula and his son David, of the
Cincinnati Bengals, became the only father-son duo ever
to face each other as head coaches in an NFL game.

One of the most versatile players in NFL history
was the St. Louis Cardinals' Chuck Latourette,
who in 1968 averaged 41.6 yards per punt
and also led the NFL in punt returns and
kickoff returns—a feat never since accomplished.

The first Super Bowl, in 1967, was called the "AFL-NFL
World Championship Game." It was held at the L.A.
Coliseum, was not sold-out, and was broadcast by both CBS
and NBC. Ticket prices for the game ranged from $6–$12,
and a total of 338 media credentials were issued to the
game. The price of a 30-second television commercial
was $42,000. By contrast, tickets to the 1999 Super Bowl
were priced at $325; 30-second commercials went for
$1.6 million; and the game was covered by 2300 media
members, broadcast to 800 million people worldwide,
covering 180 countries and 24 languages.

ASTONISHING
BUT TRUE
GOLF
STORIES

© Bettmann/CORBIS

OFF THE TEE
AND UP A TREE

Every golfer has his share of humorous or embarrassing moments while going for the prize in the heat of a tournament. As everyone who has ever hit that little round ball with any club from the bag knows, once the ball is struck, anything can happen. With a strange bounce, a wild kick off an object, or an unusual roll, the ball can wind up anywhere—even in a tree.

While most duffers would think such things only happen to them, even golf's top players have had these types of experiences.

Such was the case for two-time Masters champion Bernhard Langer early in his career. "There have been many times when crazy things have happened," he remembers.

Two of Langer's funniest memories have made golf's version of blooper reels. The first instance took place at a tournament in England in 1980. In this particular instance, Langer needed three swings of the club to hit the ball 20 yards.

"I had two air shots," Langer recalls. "I was 20 yards from the green in some heather in England. It's thick rough.

I walked in there and thought, 'Oh, it's going to be a terrible lie.' I go there [to the ball], and it's sitting right on top of this grass about a foot high. I hit right under the ball; I went under it, and the ball went down."

Langer's pitching wedge became an instant weed-whacker, and rather than hit the ball, he merely trimmed the heather. So he tried again. Once again, more heather trimming, but no ball striking.

"I hit it again and it went down. And I said to myself, 'I can't believe this. You're 20 yards away and you can't hit the ball.' So, the third time I finally hit it and got it out of there. I just shook my head and said, 'You know, this is golf.'"

There were plenty of others shaking their heads when Langer had his second experience. Once again, for a moment he was more landscaper than golfer, and he came away not only with a memory but also a new nickname. It happened during another tournament in England, this one in 1982. This time, Langer found himself up a tree—literally.

"I was playing the 17th hole when I pulled my second shot, a nine iron, to the left. I heard the ball hit a big oak tree near the green two or three times, but never saw it come down," Langer said. "As I approached the green, I could hear the spectators laughing. Sure enough, the ball was lodged up in the tree about 15 feet above the ground in a little indentation on a huge branch. I debated whether I should take the penalty shot or climb up in the tree and hit it."

What would any competitive elite professional golfer do?

"I climbed up the tree and hit it out of there and onto the green," Langer said.

Playing months later in the United States, Langer realized that word of the incident had followed him across the Atlantic Ocean.

"I heard a couple in the crowd talking about me," he remembered. "'There's the guy who was in the tree.' one spectator said. 'What's his name?' The other replied, 'I think it's Bernhard something.' 'No, it's not,' said the other. 'That's Tarzan!' I wasn't too amused at the time. But when you look back, it's quite funny."

WRONG DRIVE

In November 1991, Steve Jones crashed his dirt motorbike, spraining an ankle, separating a shoulder, and tearing ligaments in his left ring finger. Because of the damage to that one digit, that one small appendage, the career of one of golf's most promising young players was sidetracked in a big way. The injured finger would keep Jones off the PGA tour for three years and force him to make a major change in his game. Most in the golf community thought he would never come back.

"At first I thought, 'Well, you know my finger's jammed a little bit, and my shoulder hurts. I'll be back in a couple of months,'" says Jones. "Next thing I know, it was 2 ½ years before I could even swing a club. I didn't know if I was ever going to play golf again from that injury, but I didn't feel like my career was over. It took me a year to get my swing going again."

Jones switched to a reverse overlap grip to protect his finger, which will never be completely healed. At 30, this former up-and-coming star was forced to completely rebuild his game. Often, he felt like giving up. But Jones knew he still had the passion to play golf and that the talent was still there. Thousands of hours of rehabilitation and extra work finally paid off in 1996, when Jones won the U.S. Open at Bloomfield Hills, Michigan. Coming off his troubles, Jones was as unlikely an Open champion as golf had seen in years. "It was amazing to go from playing pretty well up through 1991, to all of a sudden not knowing if you're ever going to play again, to winning a major," says Jones.

Tom Lehman, who played with Jones in the final round of the '96 Open and is one of his best friends, might have been the only person besides Jones' wife, Bonnie, who wasn't surprised. "People forgot how good a player he was before he got hurt," says Lehman. "When he won it [the Open], the attitude was, 'Where did this guy come from?' But Steve proved himself a long time ago," Lehman says. "He deserves to win. He has the game to win."

Through the trials, Jones never felt sorry for himself, never caught himself asking "Why me?"

"Now, a lot of people said, 'Why do you think this happened to you?' And I said, 'Well, I know why it happened; I know why I got in a motorcycle wreck.' And they said, 'You do? Why?' And I said, 'Because I was a terrible rider.'

"I might never have won a major if I hadn't gotten injured. I definitely wouldn't have been as interesting doing interviews . . . You are going to have troubles in your life. You won't always have mountaintop experiences. The good times never last. The bad times never last. You do the best you can and move on."

IF AT FIRST
you DON'T SUCCEED

While attempting to qualify for the 1960 Portland, Oreg., City Amateur Golf Championship, Kelley Stroud amazed onlookers with his display of ineptitude and mastery.

On the par-three sixteenth hole, Stroud hit his tee shot into the water hazard. His second attempt from the tee also splashed down into the water, as did his third. As he lined up for his fourth attempt off the tee, Stroud approached his ball with six strokes to his credit for a hole on which he had not yet hit a ball into play.

On his fourth swing, Stroud hit his ball 148 yards straight into the cup, giving him an amazing four-over-par hole in one.

HEAD GAMES

Former Vice President Spiro Agnew was an avid sports fan. Stories of his escapades on the golf course made media rounds during his term as second in command to President Richard Nixon. But few moments of Agnew's sports endeavors stand out like his performance at the Bob Hope Desert Classic in 1970.

On this day, Agnew's second shot of the round hit his playing partner, pro Doug Sanders, on the head. Sanders was standing in the middle of the fairway decked out in an orange shirt, orange shoes, and green sweater. In that attire, he seemed like a target for Agnew, who did not miss. In fact, the ball hit Sanders so hard that a one-inch cut was opened up on the side of his head. He finished the hole and even managed to save par while tending to his head.

After retrieving his ball, which had ricocheted off Sanders' head and bounced out of bounds, Agnew continued to play. He sprayed balls into trees, ponds, sand traps, and groups of spectators.

After hitting another ball into the crowd on the eighth fairway, he turned to the press and said, "I'm going to kill somebody."

The following year, Agnew was allowed to participate in the Hope Classic again, although some locals were concerned for their physical safety. They weren't mistaken in their caution, as this time, Agnew hit three spectators with his first two shots.

The first ball hit 66-year-old G.L. Decker on the forehead, then caromed off and hit Decker's wife on the arm. Agnew graciously kissed the woman's arm, then teed his ball up again. His second shot went awry also and hit a woman on the ankle, sending her to the hospital for X-rays. From that point on, Hope's monologues were dotted with references to Agnew's propensity for putting fans in danger.

Incidentally, in-between his two showings at Hope's tournament, Agnew took the opportunity to see how many tennis fans he could terrorize.

Playing in a benefit tournament at the Washington Hilton, Agnew was paired with Peace Corps Director Joseph Blatchford in the doubles competition. The Vice President managed to send his second serve right onto the back of Blatchford's head. Blatchford staggered to the sidelines where in good-natured fashion, he donned a motorcycle helmet for the remainder of the game.

Amid the laughter that ensued, one fan yelled out, "What else can he play where he can bean somebody?"

MOON SHOT

February 15, 1971, stands as a momentous day in history. Not only was it a day man walked on the moon, it was also the day that saw the longest golf shot in history. The two events occurred in the same place.

Astronaut Alan Shepard was a golf fanatic. The first American launched into outer space, Shepard was commander of the Lunar Landing Mission in 1971. Upon boarding the spacecraft, Shepard managed to sneak in a cut-down 6-iron and two golf balls. When the lunar module landed on the moon six days after the Apollo 14 crew launched into space, Shepard became the 5th American to walk on the moon. He decided to play a little golf while he was there.

Shepard had managed to rig a club from four pieces of aluminum and his piece of 6-iron. He had two obstacles—his spacesuit was so big and bulky that he had to swing his "club" with just one arm. The lie wasn't very good either, with the moon's surface being like a giant sand trap.

He scuffed his first shot, yet because of the moon's atmosphere, it traveled about 200 yards. He shanked his second shot and then threw his club. Still Shepard recalled

the experience fondly. "The ball went miles and miles and miles," he said following the shot.

Comedian Bob Hope recalled something else from Shepard's walk back to the module.

"Something lying in the dust caught his eye," Hope recalled. "It was another golf ball, with Jerry Ford's name on it."

WHEN I WANT
YOUR OPINION,
I'LL ASK FOR IT

G olfer Tommy Bolt was one of the finest pro players in the 1940s and '50s. He was well-known for his sweet swing and tempestuous attitude. So mercurial was his temper, at times it got the best of him. Attempting to enliven a golf clinic one day, Bolt asked his teenaged son to "show the nice folks what I taught you." His son excitedly grabbed a 9-iron and threw it into the sky.

During one tournament, the impatient Bolt found himself joined by a caddy who was known around golf circles for his constant talking during rounds.

Bolt would have none of the chatter from the caddy and let him know about it. Before he teed off to start the round, Bolt ordered the caddy not to speak at all during the entire day unless Bolt asked him a question; and then, the caddy was told he could only answer with a yes or no.

On one hole, after an errant tee shot, Bolt found his ball lying next to a tree. Surveying his situation, Bolt saw that he would be required to hit the ball under a branch and over a lake to get the ball onto the green. He got down on his knees and looked through the trees, sizing up the shot. Then he turned to his caddy and asked him a question.

"What do you think? 5-iron?" asked Bolt.

"No, Mr. Bolt," the caddy said.

"What do you mean not a 5-iron?" Bolt snarled. "Watch this shot."

The caddy held firm. "No, Mr. Bolt."

Bolt hit the ball anyway, and hit it well, placing it within a few feet of the pin. He then turned to his caddy and handed him the 5-iron. "Now what do you think about that?" he asked. "Go ahead, you can talk now."

"Mr. Bolt," replied the caddy, "that wasn't your ball."

A REAL LONG SHOT

ntil the rules were changed in 1952, golf balls had to remain where they landed and players finding an opponent's ball in the way were required to loft their balls up in order to reach a hole. This was a key component for one of golf's most amazing stories.

Nearly 100 years ago, a female golfer was competing in the 1912 Shawnee Invitational for Ladies at Shawnee-on-Delaware. She took a huge swing at her ball and watched as it sailed majestically into the Binniekill River. But amazingly, the ball remained floating atop the water, making it possible for the golfer to hit it.

She leapt into a boat and set off in hot pursuit. She came in range of the ball, and stood up in the boat to take a whack at the ball. Numerous times the woman took a powerful swipe at the ball. She eventually made contact and sent the ball up onto a small beach—1.5 miles from where she had started the hole!

After jumping out of the boat, the woman prepared to tackle her next hurdle. A heavily wooded forest lay between her ball and the hole. She continued to hack away and finally put her ball in the cup—166 strokes later. That's 166 strokes, not for the entire 18 hole day, but for just the 130-yard, par 3, 16th hole.

ASTONISHING BUT TRUE GOLF TRIVIA

During the reign of Caesar, the Romans played a game resembling golf by striking a feather-stuffed ball with club-shaped branches.

The Dutch played a similar game on their frozen canals about the 15th century, with cross-country variations popular in France and Belgium at the same time.

In 1457, golf was banned in Scotland because it interfered with the practice of archery, which was vital to the defense effort. Nevertheless, the Scots continued to brave the opposition of both Parliament and church by playing the game on seaside courses called links.

Scotland boasts the world's oldest golf course,
St. Andrews, used as early as the 16th century.

The first 18-hole course in the U.S., the Chicago Golf
Club, was founded near Wheaton, Ill., in 1893.

Walter Hagen was the first full-time
tournament pro, beginning in 1919.

The National Golf Foundation estimates there
are more than 26 million golfers in the U.S.

Each year, U.S. golfers spend nearly
600 million dollars for equipment.

A maximum of 14 clubs may be used in
tournament play, most weighing 13–13 ½ ounces.

Golf courses and practice facilities in the
U.S. number about 15,000.

In 1968, Arnold Palmer was the first golfer to pass
the million-dollar mark in career earnings.

In 1988, Jack Nicklaus, the only golfer to be chosen five
times as the PGA Player of the Year, became the first
player to earn more than 5 million dollars in a career.

Sam Snead won a record 84 PGA tournaments.

Byron Nelson went 113 straight tournaments
in the 40's without missing the cut

Phil Mickelson is the only lefty to win
the U.S. Amateur event (1990).

The leading money winner on the men's golf tour
in 1936 was Horton Smith, with $7,682.

In winning the 1968 PGA Championship at age 48, Julius
Boros became the oldest man to win a major tournament.

Greg Norman's final round meltdown at the 1996
Masters occurred on April 14, which is the anniversary
of two notable tragedies: the assassination of Abraham
Lincoln in 1865, and the sinking of the Titanic in 1912.

The only man ever to play in a Masters tournament and the baseball World Series was Sam Byrd, who played in the 1931 World Series with the New York Yankees and had top five finishes at the Masters in 1941 and 1942.

Jack McGurn, a competing amateur at the 1933 Western Open, was arrested during the second round of play when it was learned he was the notorious hit man for Al Capone, known as "Machine Gun Jack."

In 1954, the USGA gave a special gift to then President Eisenhower—a putting green on the south lawn of the White House.

The great Bobby Jones was just 28 years old when he retired from competitive golf in 1930. Jones held college degrees in English Literature, engineering, and law.

Chi Chi Rodriguez was a teammate of future baseball
Hall of Famer Roberto Clemente, while playing on a
Class A minor league team in Puerto Rico in 1953.

Woodrow Wilson was known as the most avid golfer of
any U.S. president. He was known to play six rounds of
golf in a given week—in any type of weather. In winter,
he used red golf balls so he could find them in the snow.
His caddie was required to carry a flashlight for rounds
played in the evening. He once played a match that
did not end until 5 a.m.

For the movie *Tin Cup*, it took actor Kevin Costner
86 takes to hit the shot that he banks off the portable
toilet and onto the green, rolling right up to the camera
lens. The scene took nearly the entire day to film and
lasted just 10 seconds on the screen.

The top taxpayer in all of Shenzhen, China, in 2001 was none other than Tiger Woods. Woods paid $4.2 million yuan (about $500,000) in taxes on his undisclosed appearance fee during a promotional tournament. News about Woods paying more in taxes than anyone in the People's Republic of China—a country of 1.3 billion people—spread fast and made headlines all over the world. Woods found the news somewhat amusing. "That's actually pretty funny," Woods said. "But it's not that funny."

PGA MONEY LEADERS
AT TEN-YEAR INTERVALS

1955: Julius Boros, $63,121.55

1965: Jack Nicklaus, $140,752.14

1975: Jack Nicklaus, $298,149.17

1985: Curtis Strange, $542,321.00

1995: Greg Norman, $1,654,959.00

2005: Tiger Woods, $10,628,024.00

While Tiger Woods is the youngest golfer to win
The Masters, he's the oldest of the four youngest players
to win each of the four majors:

1968 British Open, won by young Tom Morris
at 17 years, 5 months

1911 U.S. Open, won by John J. McDermott
at 19 years, 10 months

1922 PGA, won by Gene Sarazen
at 20 years, 5 months

1997 Masters, won by Tiger Woods
at 21 years, 3 months

Jack Nicklaus won The Masters at 46 years, two months in 1986. Here are the five oldest PGA winners in the 1990s:

Ray Floyd: 49 years, 6 months, 1992 Doral

Hale Irwin: 48 years, 9 months, 1994 MCI

Tom Watson: 48 years, 8 months, 1998 Colonial

Ed Dougherty: 47 years, 7 months, 1995 Deposit

Tom Watson: 46 years, 9 months, 1996 Memorial

OTHER PRIZES AWARDED AT THE MASTERS
(BESIDES THE GREEN JACKET)

Gold Medal: Winner

Silver Medal and Silver Salver: Runner-up

Silver Cup: Love amateur

Silver Medal: Amateur runner-up

Crystal Vase: Each day's low score

Large Crystal Bowl: Hole in one

Pair of Crystal Goblets: Eagle

Large Crystal Bowl: Double Eagle

GOLF MAGAZINE'S 18 GREATEST GOLF HOLES IN THE WORLD

Par 3s

Banff Springs Golf Course,
Banff, Alberta, Canada: 4th hole, 192 yards

Cypress Point Club,
Pebble Beach, Calif.: 15th hole, 139 yards

National Golf Links of America,
Southampton, N.Y.: 4th hole, 197 yards

TPC at Sawgrass,
Ponte Vedra Beach, Fla.: 17th hole, 132 yards

Par 4s

Ballybunion Golf Club,
Ballybunion, County Kerry, Ireland:
11th hole, 453 yards

Bethpage State Park (Black Course),
Farmingdale, N.Y.: 5th hole, 451 yards

Merion Golf Club (East),
Ardmore, Pa.: 16th hole, 428 yards

Mid Ocean Club,
Tucker's Town, Bermuda: 5th hole, 433 yards

Pine Valley Golf Club,
Clementon, N.J.: 13th hole, 448 yards

Royal County Down Golf Club,
Newcastle, County Down, N. Ireland:
9th hole, 486 yards

Royal Melbourne Golf Club (West),
Black Rock, Melbourne, Australia:
6th hole, 450 yards

St. Andrews (Old), St. Andrews,
Fife, Scotland: 17th hole, 461 yards

Shinnecock Hills Golf Club,
Southampton, N.Y.: 14th hole, 447 yards

Southern Hills Country Club,
Tulsa, Okla.: 12th hole, 445 yards

Par 5s

Augusta National Golf Club,
Augusta, Ga.: 13th hole, 510 yards

Carnoustie Golf Links,
Carnoustie, Angus, Scotland: 6th hole, 578 yards

Durban Country Club,
Durban, Natal, South Africa: 3rd hole, 513 yards

Pebble Beach Golf Links,
Pebble Beach, Calif.: 18th hole, 548 yards

CELEBRITIES WHO HAVE SCORED A HOLE IN ONE

Clint Eastwood

Supreme Court Justice Sandra Day O'Connor

Don Zimmer

Kim Jon Il

Charles Schwab

Carlton Fisk

Joe DiMaggio

John Elway

Roger Clemens

3 Presidents: Eisenhower, Nixon, and Ford

BEST GOLF NICKNAMES

The Golden Bear (Jack Nicklaus)

Lord Byron (Nelson)

Lefty (Phil Mickelson)

Tiger (Eldrick Woods)

The Shark (Greg Norman)

Fuzzy (Frank Zoeller)

The Squire (Gene Sarazen)

Boom Boom (Fred Couples)

The Walrus (Craig Stadler)

Lumpy (Tim Herron)

El Niño (Sergio Garcia)

Slammin' Sammy (Sam Snead)

Chi Chi (Juan Rodriguez)

The Wild Thing (John Daly)

The Big Easy (Ernie Els)

Radar (Mike Reid)

The Merry Mex (Lee Trevino)

GOLFER SUPERSTITIONS

Charles Howell III always tees up the ball
in such a way that the club head will
smack the ball's brand name.

Justin Leonard will always mark with the
same coin—until he misses an easy putt.

Michael Clark II tries to wear underwear
with holes in them.

Mike Weir says he puts his putter in the toilet
overnight to wash away the "evil lip-out curse."

Jesper Parnevik will never mark his ball
with a coin faced head's up.

Payne Stewart never used a ball
after making a bogey with it.

Ernie Els is through with a ball after
hitting one birdie with it.

Tom Weiskopf used broken tees on par 3's.

Jack Nicklaus always carried three coins
in his pocket.

MULLIGANS:
GREAT GOLF QUOTES
& ANECDOTES

Once during the Bob Hope Classic at the Indian Wells Country Club, Gary Hallberg hit a shot that bounced off the cart path and bounded up on the roof of the clubhouse. By rule, Hallberg was permitted a free drop from the roof. Yet, he realized that the only clear shot he had at the green was from up on the roof. So he pulled his wedge out of his bag and dropped a perfectly struck shot on the green. From there, he sunk a par putt.

Veteran golf writer T.R. Reinman recalls meeting Phil Mickelson when the kid was just 14. Reinman bet Mickelson a Coke that he (Reinman) could hit a driving range fence 250 yards out, which he did. Then Mickelson bet him two Cokes that he (Mickelson) could do it with any club in Reinman's bag, even though the writer is right-handed and Mickelson is a lefty. Mickelson pulled out Reinman's driver, turned it so the toe of the club faced down, and smacked the ball 250 yards left-handed. The lesson? Don't bet with Mickelson when he's thirsty.

At the 1988 U.S. Women's Open, play was moving so slowly that golfer Lori Garbacz decided she would do something outlandish to make a point. At the 14th hole of the first round, she had her caddie go to a nearby pay phone and order a pizza to be delivered to her at the 17th tee. When Garbacz reached 17, the pizza was there waiting for her. Adding to her frustration, Garbacz had ample time to eat the pizza at 17, as there were two groups ahead of her waiting to tee off.

A popular practice round betting game on Tour is called "thousand-dollar-no-bogeys." The pros each commit to paying anyone in their respective foursome $1000 if they make it through the practice round without a single bogey. It's particularly tough at major venues like Scotland's Turnberry, where in 1994, Corey Pavin, Ben Crenshaw, Davis Love III, and Brad Faxon agreed to a game. Crenshaw was out on the second hole, Love on the 12th, and Pavin a couple of holes later. That left Faxon against three guys with a vested interest in seeing him blow up. Faxon, in an interview with *Golf Digest*, said that what ensued was one of the greatest times he's ever had on a golf course. "During those last four holes, the three of them were rooting against me out loud right to the point of contact. As soon as I hit my ball on 18, I offered them each a buyout for $975. Nobody took it. I made my par and they all paid me $1000. It took awhile, but I got a check from every one of them. Somebody's wife wasn't too happy though.

A New Zealand Web site that carried details on the time and date of every round played by all registered golfers in the country was closed down in 2001 when players complained that their bosses were finding out that they'd been out golfing when they were supposed to be in the office or at business meetings.

Arnold Palmer has given plenty of lessons, but none was as costly as the one he gave Davis Love III at Palmer's 1999 Bay Hill Invitational. Love, who admits to having less than lovely on-course temper tantrums, hit an errant bunker shot. His next shot, however, was right on target. He clobbered a sprinkler head with his club and sent a gusher of water into the sky. He said he deserved to be fined, and Palmer obliged with a repair bill for $175,003.50—$3.50 for parts, $175,000 for labor.

The Wilson's Sporting Goods Company sent Masters Champion Gene Sarazen to the 1954 U.S. Amateur championship at the Country Club in Detroit to observe and critique a young golfer. "He lunged at the ball, and he duck-hooked everything," Sarazen recalled. "He had to hole long putts and get up and down out of the sand to win the title. I told Wilson the kid would never amount to much." That kid was Arnold Palmer.

Champions Tour veteran Sammy Rachels called his 3-iron his "mother-in-law club." When asked why he gave the club that moniker, he replied, "It's my mother-in-law club because I want to hit it, but I can't."

Mac O'Grady began trying for his tour card in 1971 and failed at PGA Qualifying School a record 16 times before finally making it in 1982, on his 17th try. His story is a study in perseverance. During his annual attempt to become a Tour pro, O'Grady supported himself by working as a cook, dishwasher, busboy, caddie, and funeral home worker. Persistence paid off for O'Grady, as by 1990, he had won over $1 million on the Tour.

Ben Hogan never forgot the turning point of his golf career—and his life. It occurred in 1938 when he and his wife were down to their last $85. "If I didn't win money at the Oakland Open, I was through," Hogan recalled. "The night before the tournament started, someone stole the two rear wheels off my car. I had to hitch a ride to play. But I shot a 69 in the last round and tied for third. The $385 I won enabled me to put wheels back on my car and keep going." From that point on, Hogan began his rise to become one of the greatest golfers of all time.

In the first round of the 1927 British Open, Bobby Jones needed only 28 putts. He did not miss a putt under 12 feet and drained six from more than 100 feet. On the 5th hole, Jones sank a putt that was paced off at 120 feet.

In 1876, David Strath bet all comers he could negotiate the bunkers and huge greens of the Old Course at St. Andrews in fewer than 100 strokes—while playing in the dark. With only a full moon and those who took him up on the wager accompanying him, Strath shot 95 and didn't lose a single ball. In his memory, the front bunker on the 11th hole at St. Andrews was named the Strath Bunker.

ASTONISHING STUFF THEY SAY ABOUT GOLF

"Golf is more fun than walking naked in a strange place, but not much."

—Buddy Hackett

"Golf is an expensive way of playing marbles."

—G.K. Chesterton

"Golf is a game where the ball always lies poorly and the player well."

—Anonymous

"The golfer has more enemies than any other athlete. He has 14 clubs in his bag, all of them different; 18 holes to play, and all around him are sand, trees, grass, water, wind."

—Dan Jenkins

"Golf is a game in which you yell fore, shoot six, and write down five."

—*Paul Harvey*

"Golf is a game of inches. The most important are those between the ears."

—*Arnold Palmer*

"Golf is so popular simply because it is the best game in the world in which to be bad."

—*A.A. Milne, creator of Winnie the Pooh*

"Golf is a test of temper, a trial of honor, a revealer of character."

—*David Forgan*

"Golf is not a game of great shots. It's a game of the most accurate misses. The people who win make the smallest mistakes."

—*Gene Littler*

"What other people may find in poetry,
I find in the flight of a good drive."
—*Arnold Palmer*

"The three things I fear the most in golf are
lightning, Ben Hogan, and a downhill putt."
—*Sam Snead*

"I see no reason why a golf course cannot be
played in 18 birdies. Just because no one has
ever done that doesn't mean it can't be done."
—*Ben Hogan*

"Some days I wonder about practice. I've hit
about 70,000 golf balls in the last four years,
and some days I still play like an amateur."
—*Hubert Green*

"Prayer never seems to work for me on the
golf course. I think this has something to do with
my being a terrible putter."
—*Billy Graham*

"The only shots you can be dead sure of are those you've already taken."
—*Byron Nelson*

"Golf is a good walk spoiled."
—*Mark Twain*

"You drive for show and putt for dough."
—*Bobby Locke*

"Mr. Agnew, I believe you have a
slight swing in your flaw."

—*Jimmy Demaret, to playing partner VP Spiro Agnew*

"All that matters in golf is the next shot."

—*Ralph Guldahl*

"A driving range is the place where golfers go to
get all of the good shots out of their system."

—*Humorist Henry Beard*

"Give me a man with big hands, big feet, and no
brains, and I will make a golfer out of him."

—*Walter Hagen*

"I play in the low 80s. If it's any hotter than that,
I won't play."

—*Joe Louis*

"The older I get, the better I used to be."

—*Lee Trevino*

"I was three over. One over a house, one over
a patio, and one over a swimming pool."
—*George Brett (on his golf game)*

"I won't say my golf is bad, but if I started growing
tomatoes, they'd come up sliced!"
—*Miller Barber*

"The game was easy for me as a kid. I had to play
a while to find out how hard it is."
—*Raymond Floyd*

"The Masters is the only tournament
I ever knew where you choke when you
drive through the front gate."
—*Gary Player*

"You can't call it a sport. You don't run, jump,
you don't shoot, you don't pass. All you have to
do is buy some clothes that don't match."
—*Steve Sax*

"Ninety percent of the putts that fall short
don't go in."
—*Yogi Berra*

"I would like to think of myself as an athlete first,
but I don't want to do a disservice to the real ones."
—*David Duval*

"Columbus went around the world in 1492. That
isn't a lot of strokes when you consider the course."
—*Lee Trevino*

"If you think it's hard to meet new people,
try picking up the wrong golf ball."
—*Jack Lemmon*

"If I'm on the course and lightning starts, I get
inside fast. If God wants to play through, let him."
—*Bob Hope*

"I can airmail the golf ball, but sometimes
I don't put the right address on it."
—*Jim Dent*

"It took me 17 years to get 3,000 hits.
I did it in one afternoon on the golf course."
—*Hank Aaron, baseball legend*

"I'm hitting the woods just great, but I'm having
a terrible time getting out of them."
—*Harry Toscano*

GOLF SCORECARD

With more than 17,300, the United States has
more golf courses than any other country.
(Worldwide, there are an estimated 30,000 courses.)

All of Europe has just under 6,000 courses,
and China, home to over 1.2 billion people,
has just 100 golf courses.

It is estimated that more than 50 million
people worldwide play golf. Their average
score for a round is 107.

South African Gary Player figures he has flown
more than 14 million air miles over his career
and estimates he has spent the equivalent of
three-and-a-half to four years sitting on an airplane.

Golf courses are among the top five public places
in America where heart attacks most often occur.

ASTONISHING
BUT TRUE
STORIES FROM THE
WIDE WORLD
OF SPORTS

PERISTROIKA?

In 1972, the Canadians and the Russians faced off in a historic hockey series, called the Summit Series. It was a matchup between Canada's finest NHL stars and the best of the Soviet Red Army team—their Olympians. The series will long be remembered in Canada for Paul Henderson's series-winning goal, which made Henderson a national hero and household name throughout Canada.

Yet few are familiar with some of the diplomatic challenges that came with the series, at a time in which Soviet political relations with the West were a bit icy. The tension translated onto the ice rinks and the events that surrounded the series.

While visiting Moscow to play the Russians in the midst of the series, the Canadian hockey team was assigned a hotel room in the capital city which they suspected had been bugged.

Recalled Canadian superstar goal-scorer Phil Esposito, then of the NHL's Boston Bruins, "We searched the room for microphones. In the center of the room, we found a funny-looking, round piece of metal embedded in the floor, under the rug. We figured we had found the bug. We dug it out of the floor and heard a crash beneath us. We had released the anchor to the chandelier in the ceiling below."

RACING ON FUMES

Wilbur Shaw was one of the early superstars of auto racing. In the 1930s and '40s, he was the name in Indy-style racing circles. He became known not only for his driving ability but also his penchant for taking risks and more often than not, making good on those chances. He seemed to have a knack for knowing just what he had to do to win. The 1937 Indianapolis 500 is one such example.

At Indy that year, Shaw had a three-mile lead on second-place driver Ralph Hepburn, with 35 laps to go. The lead amounted to more than one lap on the two-and-one-half-mile oval. Shaw seemed to be coasting to another victory at the famed Brickyard.

But then the unthinkable happened: Shaw sprung a leak. His Maserati 8CTF began leaking oil at a rate that looked to take him out of the race. Told by his pit crew that he was one minute and fourteen seconds ahead of Hepburn, Shaw immediately calculated in his head how much he could afford to slow down to conserve oil and still finish ahead of Hepburn.

Shaw cut his speed. Hepburn quickly began to catch up. Soon, he passed Shaw to pick up the entire lap he had fallen behind and began to close the gap with every lap.

Shaw began to rethink his math, wondering if he had really calculated correctly. With every second, Hepburn made up more ground. On the last turn of the final lap, Hepburn came even with Shaw and began nosing ahead, and it looked like Indy might be lost for Shaw.

But just as Hepburn came alongside of him, Shaw accelerated, hoping there was enough oil for one last push. His Maserati gave one last chug, and then the engine gasped and quit, just as the car crossed the finish line. Amazingly, with hardly more than a drop of oil left in his engine, Shaw had edged out Hepburn in what was the closest race in Indianapolis 500 history—by 2.16 seconds.

UNITED WE STAND: DEREK REDMOND

The 1992 Summer Olympic games were destined to become one of the most touching and memorable in history. In Barcelona, Spain, site of the games, emotion was high as much of the world had just come through the tension of the Gulf War conflict. The Olympics provided an opportunity to rebuild a sense of peace and goodwill among nations. No event from the '92 games made a greater impact on the world in creating a lasting image of unity than the 400 meter semifinal race in track and field.

Derek Redmond, British track star, was a favorite to be among those on the medal podium at the end of competition. He had his heart set on receiving gold. Yet what happened to Redmond would not result in a gold medal, but rather a golden moment.

In the middle of the race, Redmond seemed to be running smoothly and preparing to set up for his kick to the finish to place himself in a prime spot to win the final. But suddenly, Redmond pulled up, grabbed for the back of his leg, and fell to the track in a crumpled heap. The dream was over. Redmond's pursuit of Olympic hardware had come to a crushing halt.

Still, Redmond was not to be defeated. With his face showing the excruciating pain caused from what he would later learn was a torn hamstring, Redmond was determined to finish the race. He rose from the track, his competitors now a hundred yards ahead, and began to hobble toward the finish line. Each step was marked by agony. The crowd gasped collectively, as if they could feel the pain Redmond was experiencing. Yet Redmond was undaunted in his desire to cross the finish line. His will was strong, but his leg could not hold out. Like a wounded animal, he attempted to continue. All eyes were on the injured runner.

Within moments, Redmond's father, Jim, jumped out of the stands and made his way toward the track. When security personnel attempted to stop him, Jim Redmond, yelled, "That's my son!" He was allowed to pass and entered the track, where he came to the aid of his son.

When he reached Derek's side, Jim grabbed his son's arm and said, "You don't have to do this."

"Yes, I do," Derek responded.

With that being said, Jim draped Derek's left arm around his own shoulders. He then placed his right arm around the shoulders of his son. Then he grabbed Derek's right arm, and began to lead him to the finish line. With his father walking beside him, Derek hopped along gingerly and completed the race. Together, slowly, father and son made it down the back stretch and reached the finish line, while an amazed crowd rose to their feet and roared with wild cheers. The image was captured by photographers and television cameras and was quickly seen around the world, in what has become one of the most emotional and inspiring moments in Olympic history.

The official results of the men's 400 meter semifinal race show Derek Redmond's performance as "race abandoned." The world will remember it as anything but. Rather, this race will long be remembered as a unifying moment that sport has rarely seen—when a father and son came together to finish the race, in one of the most remarkable displays of teamwork in sports history.

SUPER SPORTSMANSHIP: EUGENIO MONTI

The 1964 Olympic Winter Games in Innsbruck, Austria, became the site of one of the greatest displays of sportsmanship the world of sports has ever seen. It was there that bobsledding legend Eugenio Monti showed the world what the true spirit of competition is all about.

The Bobsled competition looked to be one of the most highly competitive events in all of the games. In the four-man Bobsled event, the hometown Austrians and the Italians, led by the legendary Monti, were thought of as the clear favorites for gold. The Canadian team was expected to compete for the bronze medal, with an outside chance of finishing higher. But an amazing story unfolded that would forever mark the landscape of sports and competition.

On their run in the first heat, the Canadian team broke the Olympic record and held a substantial lead of one-half of a second over the rest of the field. However, on that record setting run, the Canadians encountered a problem. Their sled went into the last turn too fast, hit the ice wall, and damaged the axle. If they couldn't fix it, they would be disqualified.

Monti did not want to win the event unless he was able to race against each competitor at his best and compete on equal terms. Fifteen minutes before their next run, the Canadian team's Victor Emery reached the top of the track to find his sled upside down. In an incredible act of sportsmanship, the Italians had taken the sled apart and Monti's mechanics were fixing it. With Monti's help, the Canadians were not only able to race but also to stay in the lead and win the gold. Monti and his team had to settle for the bronze.

Later, in the two-man Bobsled event, Monti's character was on display once again. Tony Nash of Great Britain, after his first run, had recorded the fastest time. But the bolt attaching the sled's runners to the vehicle's shell had sheared. Monti, who was at the top of the course about to steer the Italian team's sled down the track when he learned of the incident said, "Get an Englishman and a spanner to the finish, and they can have my bolt." Monti even offered to withdraw from the race if it was the only way he could loan Nash his bolt. True to his word and ignoring questioning from startled Italian journalists, Monti had the bolt from his sled taken off and sent back up the hill to the start line, where it was quickly attached to Nash's sled just in time for his run. Once again, Monti's actions proved heroic for his opponents. The team of Nash and Robin Dixon took home the gold for Great Britain, and Monti again won the bronze.

When the games were over, Monti was honored for his amazing display of respect with the first Pierre de Coubertin Award for Sportsmanship. But not everyone was happy about Monti's display of respect for his competitors. He was viciously attacked in the Italian newspapers, but nevertheless remained steadfast. "Nash didn't win because I gave him the bolt," he said. "He won because he had the fastest run."

Monti eventually won his gold medal, as well. At age 40, at the 1968 Grenoble Winter Olympic Games, he took the gold in *both* the two-man and four-man Bobsled events. He completed his storied career with six Olympic medals—the two gold and two bronze—along with two silvers he earned at the 1956 Cortina, Italy, Games. Monti also won nine world championships and gained the nickname "Il Rosso Volante," or The Red Flyer. Recently, award-winning Olympic historian and filmmaker Bud Greenspan, in partnership with General Motors, honored Monti as the 3rd Greatest Winter Olympian, in any sport, of all-time. "Eugenio Monti is deserving of the title as the Greatest Bobsled Driver in history," said Greenspan. "His career was significant, and his gesture of friendship and good sportsmanship in 1964 has been an inspiration for all who compete at the Olympic Games."

His respect for his competitors and his willingness to put others first earned Eugenio Monti a prominent place in Olympic history. He was a representation of sportsmanship at its best by pursuing victory with honor.

FINISHING STRONG: JOHN STEPHEN AKHWARI

The year was 1968. The place was Mexico City, site of the '68 Summer Olympic games. It happened late one night in the main track and field stadium.

Out of the cold darkness, John Stephen Akhwari from Tanzania entered the stadium at the far end. He hobbled slowly and unsteadily. Pain filled every step. Blood ran down his bandaged leg. His dreams of Olympic glory faded in the shadows of the night.

Over an hour earlier, the winner of the Olympic marathon had already been declared. All other runners had completed the 26.2 miles shortly thereafter. Only a few spectators remained in their seats. There was no cheering, no flag waving. Yet the lone runner pressed on.

As he neared the Olympic Stadium, word circulated that there was one runner still on the course. Other Olympians and spectators quickly came back to the stadium to watch the scene unfold. The stadium lights flickered back on again. Akhwari entered the stadium and began to wearily pound out his final lap around the track. As Akhwari neared the finish line, the small crowd that had gathered began to roar with appreciation. They stood and cheered the lone runner all the way to the finish line. After crossing the white stripe, an exhausted Akhwari nearly collapsed. Yet in his anguish, he managed to exhibit an expression of determined achievement as he acknowledged the faithful few who had witnessed his final steps.

After it was all over, a reporter asked Akhwari why he had not retired from the race, as he had fallen so far back and had no chance of winning.

Akhwari seemed confused by the question, but finally answered.

"My country did not send me 5,000 miles to Mexico City to start the race," he said. "They sent me 5,000 miles to finish the race."

ABOUT THE AUTHOR

Steve Riach is a principal and founder of SER Media, a Dallas-based media company. He is an award-winning producer, writer, and director of numerous television, film, documentary, and video projects and is one of the nation's foremost creators of virtuous and positive-themed sports content. Steve's programs have been seen on ESPN, FOX Sports, NBC, and a variety of broadcast and cable television outlets. He is also the principal behind the creative vision for the Heart of a Champion® brand. His start in sports media came as an on-air personality, hosting national television and radio programming.

A prolific writer, Steve has authored *Passion for the Game; Above the Rim; The Drive to Win; Inspire a Dream; It's How You Play the Game; Life Lessons from Auto Racing; Life Lessons from Golf; Life Lessons from Baseball; Heart of a Champion: Profiles in Character; Amazing But True Sports Stories; Amazing Athletes Amazing Moments; Par for the Course;* and *Girl Power.*

Steve is also the cofounder of the Heart of a Champion Foundation, a nonprofit organization devoted to producing materials designed to instill character and ethics in youth. Steve is creator and author of the foundation's innovative Heart of a Champion® Character Development Program, a leading tool for the character education of students in schools, after-school outlets, and juvenile justice programs across America.

A former college baseball player and a cancer survivor, Steve is also a sought-after speaker to education groups, youth agencies, schools, corporations, sports organizations, and faith-based organizations.

A native of Southern California, Steve and his family now make their home in Colleyville, Texas.

If you have enjoyed this book
or it has touched your life in some way,
we would love to hear from you.

Please send your comments to:
Hallmark Book Feedback
P.O. Box 419034
Mail Drop 215
Kansas City, MO 64141

Or e-mail us at:
booknotes@hallmark.com